THE Victorious LIFE

THE Victorious LIFE

CHARLES KALIMA

THE Victorious LIFE

First Edition, First Impression, 2021
ISBN 978-1-990935-40-4

Copyright © Charles Kalima

Contact information:
Charles Kalima
Life in the Word Church
Tel: +27 (0)10 100 8465
PO Box 21070, Helderkruin, 1733
Email: info@litwordc.org
Website: www.litwordc.org

Published by Zion Publications
Content Layout And Typesetting by Zion Publications

Contact information:
Zion Publications
Email: info@zionintl.com
Website: http://www.zionintl.com

All scripture quotations are from the King James Version of the Bible unless otherwise stated.

© All rights are reserved. Apart from any fair dealing for the purpose of research, criticism or review as permitted under the Copyright Act, no part of this publication may be reproduced, stored in a retrieval system or transmitted, in any form or by any means, electronic, mechanical, photocopying, recording, or otherwise, without the prior written permission of the copyright holder.

CONTENTS

INTRODUCTION i

CHAPTER 1:
Victory Guaranteed 1

CHAPTER 2:
Be Sure To Believe Right 11

    A. God Does Not Bring Calamity? 16

    B. God Is Not Always In Control 28

    C. The Holy Spirit Is With You Forever 39

    D. Fear Is A Spirit 46

    E. The Body And Blood Of The Lord Jesus 51

    F. The Favour Of God Is Available To All 56

    G. God Does Not Take Away Good Things From Us .. 63

    H. Pray And Never Give Up 66

CHAPTER 3:
You Are Permanently In The Lord 73

CHAPTER 4:
Victory Belongs To You In The Lord Jesus 79

CHAPTER 5:
You Must Be Born Again 93

CHAPTER 6:
Step Up To God's Glory 103

CHAPTER 7:
Find The Thief 117

CHAPTER 8:
Love Your Way To Victory 123

CHAPTER 9:
Your Faith Overcomes The World 129

BIBLIOGRAPHY 143

OTHER BOOKS BY THE AUTHOR 145

INTRODUCTION

Every human being, on the face of this Earth, has the ability to live a victorious life. It is not for a select few; it is for all. This victory is not over other human beings. You cannot have victory over someone you are not contending with. The Bible says we do not contend against people. Therefore, we do not measure our success based on other people. We have a standard of God's Word that is our measuring stick. We are masters of satan, demons and everything that God has created – other than human beings, of course.

It is a God-given blessing, upon all, to be successful and to be able to dominate every circumstance and always come out on top of things. When God created the human race, the Bible says that He blessed them

> ***And God blessed them, and God said unto them, Be fruitful, and multiply, and replenish***

> *the earth, and subdue it: and have dominion over the fish of the sea, and over the fowl of the air, and over every living thing that moveth upon the earth.*
> **Genesis 1:28 KJV**

God's blessing upon mankind, in its entirety, still stands today. We have made use of the blessing to multiply and we have increased in number by having children. But there is more to that, as the fall of Adam did not make it any less than what God had intended it to be. Many people have accepted the blessing to multiply through childbearing but have ignored the blessing to subdue the Earth. We have accepted that childbearing is part of nature and we make plans to have a family at a certain age. This level of certainty, with having children, must be the level of certainty with becoming materially prosperous in life. Childbearing and material prosperity are both part of the blessing that God pronounced on mankind. The Earth and sea are the source of all types of industry that you can think of. Dominating these, therefore, means that we become owners of the Earth and sea-initiated industries. God further gives us dominion over every living thing and empowers us to own livestock. God did not leave anything out in order to make us be absolute masters over His creation. He gave it all to us. When God blessed man, what did He mean? He empowered man to prosper; to be made wealthy and successful in every area of human existence. **Proverbs 10:22** says:

> *The blessing of the LORD establishes wealth,*
> *and difficulty does not accompany it.*
> *Proverbs 10:22 ISV*

We must understand that when God pronounced a blessing upon mankind, He loaded man with the ability to become successful in everything that he was required to do on this Earth. Men and women, who have realised that they are blessed by the God Who made the Heavens and the Earth, have gone ahead in life to accomplish great things against all odds. They have not only achieved great things and overcome the most difficult challenges, but they have also influenced others to change their way of thinking. They have encouraged children to think and embrace victory and not defeat, success and not failure, life and not death, faith and not fear. Every human being is created to win and destined for victory. The men and women who are settled in the understanding that they are wired for success, will experience stumbling blocks in life, but they will not stumble over them; instead they will use them as stepping stones for their next level of growth. Nothing beats a person who knows and understands that the blessing of God is too big for them to fail.

God is so focused on making humans fruitful that He is willing to get involved in the life of anyone who is unfruitful. He wants to help. You may ask, *"Why don't the people, who are suffering today, see the invisible hand of God wanting to lift them out of their dire straits?"* The Bible gives an answer to this question. God says, *"My people are destroyed for lack of knowledge"* (Hosea 4:6).

Another point to note, from the verse of Scripture we quoted above in Genesis, is that the blessing was given to both male and female. God has empowered both male and female, with the same capabilities, to dominate everything He made. Women don't belong in the kitchen, they belong in the marketplace and are equal partners in achieving great things for the benefit of man.

In this book, I want to show you that you have the capacity and capability in you, no matter what your background is or what your physical limitations are, to succeed in life and to accomplish whatever you set your mind on to do. With this mentality, you need to aim high and relentlessly pursue every dream that you have, with everything God has given to you. God will see to it that you succeed. All you need to

INTRODUCTION

do is rise up and start doing something. Doors do not open to people who sit down and wish for things. They open to those who get up and head for the place they desire to obtain, and knock. They do not knock once but they keep on knocking until the door opens. The Lord Jesus said, *"...to him who knocks, the door will be opened."*

One problem, with some people, is that they do not take time to understand what they need and if it has been given to them by God. They start to pursue goals that have not been thought out and established in their being. When difficulties come, they throw in the towel and give up. It is good to take time to think about the goal you would like to pursue, especially if it is not clear that it has been given to you in Scripture. Think about it and consider all the pros and cons that are related to achieving that goal. Consider the cost and be satisfied, within yourself, that you want that for your life. Then bring it before God, in prayer, and summon every fibre of your being to see it come to pass.

A victorious life is a life of dominion, success and a positive outlook in life. When we talk *victory*, we refer to every step forward; to overcome challenges in life, which makes us assured of our dominant status and gets us into a position that is better than our previous position. Our lives are made to progress. To move from one place of success to a higher one.

While the blessing is upon every human on Earth, the Lord Jesus came to re-enforce our human ability, by giving us divine ability. You see, the assignment of mankind, at creation, was limited to domination over the creation of God, not over human beings. Sin entered the world and then the Lord Jesus came into the world to put away sin, by sacrificing Himself. He then gave His followers additional responsibilities, which were for reaching other people with His Gospel. He said that you shall receive power, after the Holy Spirit has come upon you, and you shall be my witnesses (**Acts 1:8**). The natural man could not achieve this new assignment, therefore, the Lord had to capacitate us with the divine power of the Holy Spirit living in us. The moment you receive the Lord Jesus as your personal Saviour and Lord, you are raised to a place of power and authority, which flows from God into you. You must then seek the baptism in the Holy Spirit. You will walk from one place of victory to the other, as you continue in the Word of God and stay connected to the Lord Jesus in prayer. The Holy Spirit becomes your constant Guide. He speaks to your spirit and gives direction to your mind. As long as you walk in the light of the Word of God, you will remain undefeated. Even with those battles that seem like they have defeated you, God will turn them into greater victories for you. You may have failed an examination, but that failure will be turned into success. Our God works out all things

INTRODUCTION

for good to those who love Him and are called according to His purpose. If you seem to have lost what rightfully belongs to you, do not be discouraged; lift up your head to the God – Who can never lie – Who promised you what seems to have been lost. He may say to you, *"Pursue and you will recover all,"* or He may say to you, *"Let it go and turn to look at what else I have given to you."* God will tell you to pursue irreplaceable things, like your loved ones and you are guaranteed to recover all. Possessions, on the other hand, may be let go; God may ask you to turn away from them and to let them go. In this instance, He will give you something even better. When Ziklag was invaded and women and children taken by the Amalekites, David inquired of the Lord what his plan of action was to be. God told him to pursue the Amalekites and recover whatever was taken away. Abraham, on the other hand, had to let go of his right as the elder statesman over Lot. He allowed Lot to choose the land of his settlement before him. He did this for the sake of peace between him and his nephew, Lot.

Of course, there will be times when the things you are trying to do, do not work. Do not take it as defeat; take it as a learning opportunity. When you have set out to accomplish something and that thing seemingly falls flat, you either get a second chance so you can try doing it better or you will move onto something better. Sometimes the things people try to do, do not work because they did not give their best. The blessing of God is not a licence to be lazy and then expect that good things will fall on your lap, as you lazy around. You have to work hard. Make sure that you give your greatest effort, in every attempt, at achieving something great. You may fail at your first attempt but do not give up. Rise up and go for it again. At times we fail to achieve something because we embark with a mentality of *trying*. If you are going after a business deal just to try it out, you have already braced yourself for failure. Never set off on an important journey just to **try it out**. Set on your quest, for success, to **do it**. People with a *try* mentality, always end up saying, *"I tried it and it was not for me."* Go to school in order to make the best of it. Start music lessons, aiming to **do it** and become the best that you can be. If you get into anything and want to *try* it out, you are wasting valuable time and it is better that you do not do it at all; rather find something that you will do with your whole heart.

When you set out to do a certain project, do not have other alternatives; make that project the one and only thing that you are focusing, on at the time, and put all your energy in it in order to succeed. Even if you seem to fail in achieving it, that failure will not make you lose interest and stop pursuing the project. Double mindedness is a drawback to success. The Bible says that a double minded person is unstable in all his ways (James 1:8). Always have one type of project at a time. Unless you are pursuing multiple projects that are not an alternative to each other. Do proper planning and consultation, where necessary, before you embark on your project. If the project turns out not to be feasible, it may as well be that your planning of consultation was not comprehensive.

I have always been an enthusiast of industrialisation. So, when a friend of mine, from China, asked that we collaborate on an electric vehicle project, which would include local assembly in Zambia, I jumped at the opportunity and accepted the offer. I set up a sales and marketing team for these electric vehicles in Lusaka and we started our government stakeholder engagements. Every stakeholder, that we engaged with, welcomed the idea and, based on this, we went ahead and brought in two electric vehicles to start the project. When we took them to the relevant authorities for registration, we were told of one important stakeholder that we did not consult with – the legislature. At the time, Zambian laws did not make provision for vehicles without an engine capacity in terms of Cubic Centimetres (CCs) to be registered in the country. With this roadblock, my project stalled. I had to change course to gasoline vehicles, while we waited for the law to be amended. But the project is still in the cards.

I also repeated grade seven three times and only passed on my third attempt. It was common for young people in my day to fail grade seven once, and then they would give up and drop out of school. I did not drop out, after at my first failed attempt, nor at my second failed attempt. I went on for my third attempt because my school story was set in my mind. I had to go all the way and obtain a university degree. My friends, who dropped out of school, went ahead and got married and started doing business. They had more money than me, but my mind was not distracted. That was their choice and mine was different. I was set like a flint towards my goal to achieve a university degree. If I had passed on my first or second attempt, I could have gone on to do my high school years at a provincial school, which, at the time, did not have a high pass rate for a university entry. The third attempt, however, opened the door for me to be selected to do high school at a national technical school, where I had the opportunity to be taught by some of the best local and international teachers that Zambia had at the time. University entry, from this school, was almost a given.

My university journey was also not without its own challenges. I failed twice and had to repeat the subjects I failed, for an entire year. This threw me back by two years. Today, I joke with my wife that I had to stay longer at the university to meet her. The truth is that I could not have met my beautiful wife, if I had not stayed at the university a bit longer. The lesson here, is that I did not lose my vision to obtain a university degree, despite all the challenges I went through.

When projects involve other people, you can only push it so far when it comes to trying to get them to support your way of thinking. There comes a time when certain associations should be let go of, so you can move onto greater things in life.

There are people that you need to learn to say, *"Goodbye,"* to because continuing with them may limit your growth. Abram had to part ways with his nephew, Lot, because there was not enough land available for each of them to expand on (**Genesis 13**). Lot and Abram's herdsmen started to fight amongst each other for resources. When fighting for resources starts happening in a relationship, it is a good sign in knowing that it is time to separate and that each party must move on. There are also times when certain individuals do not have the capacity to raise a leader out of the child born to them. The father of Moses was one of these people. God arranged for Moses to be raised by someone who would teach him leadership characteristics, which were required of him in order to lead the children of Israel out of Egypt. His father could only teach him how to be an obedient slave, so as to avoid the lashes of the slave masters. But this was not God's intent for Moses. You could be in a relationship where one person is only bent on training you to be a slave and does not see the potential that you have. They abuse you and every time you try to do something great for yourself, they discourage you and try to humiliate you. You may as well let go of that relationship and let God do greater things in your life. In today's world, we find a lot of men oppressing women and girls, because they believe that they have the God-given right to be masters, while the women remain as slaves. If you know a man like this, show them what God says in **Genesis 1**:

> *So, God created man in his own image, in the image of God created he him; male and female created he them. And God blessed them, and God said unto them, Be fruitful, and multiply, and replenish the earth, and subdue it: and have dominion over the fish of the sea, and over the fowl of the air, and over every living thing that moveth upon the earth.*
> *Genesis 1:27-28 KJV*

Notice here that the blessing to subdue the Earth was given to both male and female. Women and men are both blessed to become leaders of organisations that exploit Earth's resources, for the benefit of mankind. As a woman, you can be victorious and in your leadership role, you can be a leader of a Christian ministry or a circular organisation and have men as your subordinates. Do not let anyone subdue you. There is a book for women, which I have started thinking of writing. For now, let us go back to your victorious life, whether you are a male or female.

The Lord Jesus gave us a formula to be able to live in victory, even when we seem to be facing defeat. This is what He had to say:

> *You have heard that it was said, "An eye for an eye, and a tooth for a tooth." But I say to you, Do not resist evil. But whoever shall strike you on your right cheek, turn the other to him also. And to him desiring to sue you, and to take away your tunic, let him have your coat also. And whoever shall compel you to go a mile, go with him two. Give to him who asks of you, and you shall not turn away from him who would borrow from you.*
> *Matthew 5:38-42 MKJV*

This lesson I want to draw from this, is that we must always be in control. The following extract from Albert Barnes Notes, on the Bible, is worth mentioning, before we proceed:

The general principle which he laid down was, that we are not to resist evil; that is, as it is in the Greek, nor to set ourselves against an evil person who is injuring us. But even this general direction is not to be pressed too strictly. Christ did not intend to teach that we are to see our families murdered, or be murdered ourselves; rather than to make resistance. The law of nature, and all laws, human and divine, justify self-defense when life is in danger. It cannot surely be the intention to teach that a father should sit by coolly and see his family butchered by savages, and not be allowed to defend them. Neither natural nor revealed religion ever did, or ever can, inculcate this doctrine. Our Saviour immediately explains what he means by it. Had he intended to refer it to a case where life is in danger, he would most surely have mentioned it. Such a case was far more worthy of statement than those which he did mention[1].

When someone stronger than you seems to be imposing themselves on you, where they treat you cruelly, and you

---

1 Albert Barnes' Notes on the Bible, 1847-85

have no opportunity for self-defence, it may look like you have been overpowered. But the Lord Jesus says something very profound here, which will nullify the aggressor's claim of victory over you. He says that when they strike you on the left cheek, give them the right cheek as well. You see this nullifies the aggressor's claim of victory over you. If they aggressively take control and impose themselves, and you have no chance of defending yourself in stopping them, then you should let them strike you on the other cheek as well. The second-strike shifts control from them to you. You are now the victor, and you are now the person in control of the situation. When someone asks something from you, even when you only have enough to fill your own belly, share the same with them. Do not turn them away and think that you will be in need because you become more blessed when you give, than when you receive (**Acts 20:35**).

CHAPTER 1

VICTORY GUARANTEED

The creation of Adam and Eve was God's idea. God decided to make these human beings from the dust of the ground and bring them into existence in this world. God's method has changed but His role, as Creator of mankind, has not. God is still responsible for commissioning the introduction of every human being into this world. In fact, we all have the same mandate that was given to Adam and Eve – to be fruitful, multiply, replenish, subdue and to have dominion. Nothing here talks about defeat for anyone of God's creations. Of course, we know that Adam and Eve sinned against God. They sold out to the devil and sin and the curse entered the world. But the Lord Jesus came and delivered us from the curse of sin and the curse of the law. He raised us up to a position of authority, higher than where we could have been through Adam. We are now seated with Him, at the right hand of the Father – a place of authority and victory. Praise God. So, we have both the first blessing pronounced on Adam, as well as the blessings that come with receiving the Lord Jesus as our Saviour and Lord.

It is your God-given right to be fruitful – fruitfulness is the opposite of bareness. God's will for all His children is that whatever they do, they will prosper (Psalm 1:3). He is only thinking thoughts of success about you. His plans for you are also plans of prosperity in whatever you do. So, you must approach every project in life with the knowledge that you will succeed. You will obtain good grades at school. You are empowered by God to reproduce in your body, in your businesses and bear tangible results with every work you put your hands to. Fruitfulness and multiplication go together. They both do not start from a zero base. The initial gifts and talents have already been given to every person by God. Your physical and intellectual capabilities are your first assets. You can use them to make profit or make a success of your life. You must also take advantage of the opportunities that are presented to you wherever you are. You can then start growing and changing your position from where you are to something better. There is something you must plant or something that you must put your hands to. It talks about work – hard work. Work is part of the blessing that God has given us. It helps us step into greater victories in life. You might be in prison and your next level of victory is freedom. Even in that place, there are things that you need to start doing in order to get yourself into a place of freedom. Listen to your inward man – this is the part of you that makes contact with God. God will drop an idea in your spirit, which will help you get out of a place of utter desperation into victory. The point is that you must work on it. Obey the inward voice and do the dictates of your heart, so that you can see yourself walking on the path to success.

If you decide to depend on peoples' recommendations, you will not get anywhere. You must decide to do it all alone. People are great to have around you, to encourage you, but there are times when the world has stereotyped you and placed you in a *good for nothing* category. In that circumstance, be sure to believe in yourself and the abilities that God has given to you. You must understand that God places a mandate on every person that He has created. People may judge you based on their definition of acceptable conduct, but your mandate may not be what everyone else calls *normal*. God once told the Prophet Isaiah, *"My thoughts are not your thoughts…"* (**Isaiah 55:8**). The more people think that you are different, the more unique God's assignment is for you on this Earth. You may fail to achieve passing grades so that you can go to University, but that may not be the measure of your success. School is very important for all of us. However, there are people who are wired differently and the learning method, in most schools, will not be suitable for them. Failing to achieve University entry is not the end of the world. There are many other avenues of victory that a person can pursue. Just listen to your heart and whatever your heart is leading you to do, do it with all your might. As indicated earlier, if failure comes as a distraction from your goal, then get up and do it again. Never stop until you succeed. However, if failure comes because you are in the wrong field, get out as quickly as possible and find your place.

> ***Before I formed you in the womb I knew you; and before you were born I sanctified you, and I ordained you a prophet to the nations.***
> ***Jeremiah 1:5 MEV***

God is saying to each one of us, *"Before I formed you, in the womb, I knew you."* Before you were born, the whole Godhead sat in counsel and said, *"Let us make Charles. His mandate shall be an encourager."* This is what God said about Jeremiah. Jeremiah's assignment was to be a prophet to the nations. God blesses whatever we do. But we need to narrow down our activities to one specific thing that we must perfect and be the best that we can be in that. God called Jeremiah to be a prophet only. He was not a prophet, king, and priest. King David is one of the few people who operated in all three offices. But he also had one dominant one, by which he was identified – he was a king. You have heard the phrase, *"Jack of all trades but master of none."* This is not best model for success. You need to identify one area of calling that makes you stand out. You may have other projects running but your calling must be clear, so that you can be the best at it.

God wants us to be diligent in whatever we do in life. That is why He says, *"Whatever you do in word or deed, do it as if you are doing it for the Lord."* (Colossians 3:17 paraphrased). You will not be sloppy when you are doing things for the Lord. The same energy and diligence must be applied to ordinary activities, which will get us out of poverty. Too many believers are praying to get out of debt or to become rich and successful, but their work ethics contradict their prayers. The blessing of the Lord is to cause increase of the things you do. The results of multiplication depend on the figures you start with. If you start with zero, it does not matter how many times you multiply it, the answer will always be zero. You must therefore have something for God to multiply. He blesses the works of your hands and, therefore, if your hands have done no work, there will be nothing that God can bless. Remember that God's job, in our partnership with Him to make us victorious and successful, is to cause the increase. Like Paul says in

1 Corinthians 3:6, *"I planted, and Apollos watered but it is God who causes the increase."* If the seed is not planted and watered, there will be nothing for God to increase. My message to you, is that you need to get up, and start using the strength and wisdom that God has given you in order to bring you a victorious Christian life. God has given you an important head start that you need in life – the blessing. When God told Abraham to leave his ancestral home, he left with nothing but the blessing of God. The blessing opened doors of favour, brought increase, and until he was very successful.

You do not have to live a life of regret over things that you have no control over - like family. God decided which family you would be born into. He also decided which man would carry your physical makeup in his loins. Your earthly father only gave you your physical identity, which is not the real you. You are a spirit. You have been created in the image and likeness of God, and the Bible says, *"God is a Spirit"* (**John 4:24**). So, if we are in God's image then we are also spirits. Our earthly fathers cannot give us their spiritual identity. You could look like your father physically, but your spirit and his spirit are different. Our physical DNA connects us to our earthly parents and siblings. But our spiritual DNA is different. You can be brothers and sisters, but your spiritual identity is different. Uniquely made by God, to fulfil a different role in this world. God gave you your spirit and He also gave you your actual identity, because you are a spirit and the Bible says that God is the Father of spirits (**Hebrews 12:9**). If your earthly father became disobedient and used violent means in order to father the person that they were commanded to father, this does not take away God's mandate and assignment on that person. Shake off every physical limitation that locks you into your physical heritage and look at the abundant heritage you have in your Heavenly Father.

You could have been conceived in sin, like David was (**Psalm 51:5**), but that does not, in any way, lessen God's mandate on your life and His commitment to help you achieve it. You are still God's masterpiece, commissioned to be born, by God Himself, and created to achieve great things for God and for His glory. If an ungodly method of conception was used such as rape, the mistake is not the child's, but rather the method that your father chose to conceive you. The *decision* to have you conceived by the same man whose child you are, was right, but the *method* could have been wrong. Your father could have done the *normal thing* of marrying a woman and then conceiving you; or maybe he did not do that and he was disobedient before God and he chose an ungodly way to do it. You are precious in the sight of God and you have been destined to achieve great things, no matter how you came into this world. People who decide to terminate an unwanted pregnancy are punishing the unborn child with death, for the mistake or sin of someone else. Is that really fair? Should the right to life be less important than the right to comfort? Every child has the right to life, no matter how their conception took place.

Just to take a short side journey here. There are many fathers who have perverted their God-given assignments in bringing forth children, into this world, in a godly manner. There are also many other people, who have perverted their God-given assignments in order to do things for God's glory. We have preachers everywhere who are not preaching the Word of God but, rather, gossiping – a gossiper is a perverted preached or counsellor. They are interested in other peoples' lives; not to counsel them but to *skinner* on them. You will find many types of God-given gifts that are perverted.

The key thing to realize, is that no matter how you came into this would, you are God's special treasure. Your parents may have called you an unwanted child, but they are wrong. You were thought of by God, to come into existence exactly when you did. And you came into this world for a special purpose.

CHAPTER 1

As we continue in this book, to explore the areas of victory that are ours in the Lord Jesus, we must keep in mind that there is no one who is excluded from living a victorious life. Everyone, from children born from rich parents to those born on the street. All can experience victory in this life. I saw street children turned to become responsible young men when they received the gospel of the Lord Jesus. This happen in the street of Lusaka where we were ministering to street boys. Our meetings took place right in the city centre of Lusaka. This place attracted many street children who came to the church. I used to go and round them up and bring them into our venue, to teach them the Word. Some of the children understood the Word and gave their lives to the Lord Jesus. I then left Lusaka for work in Johannesburg and when I returned to Lusaka, I was told that a number of these children had become responsible married men. I remember one boy who had one of his eyes poked out, while on the streets, during a street fight. This boy gave his life to the Lord. The Lord has raised him to be a leader in a church and is a businessman, who now has a family. God's Word works for anybody.

.

The victorious life is not just for the people born with a silver spoon in their mouths. It is also for the ordinary person. Our job is to preach this Gospel of the Lord Jesus to everyone. The Gospel of the Lord Jesus is the blessing, which makes rich. When the Lord Jesus announced His ministry in Luke 4, He said that He was anointed to preach the Gospel to the poor (v18). Why the poor? Because God is concerned about our physical welfare, as much as He is for our spiritual welfare. The Gospel is the blessing. When it is preached to and received by the poor, the poor are made rich.

In the next chapters, I will explain some of the things you need to do in order to live a victorious life. These lessons are what we would call in the automotive industry, "Where the rubber hits the road." Enjoy.

CHAPTER 2
BE SURE TO BELIEVE RIGHT

One of the biggest areas of defeat, for many people, is wrong believing. If you believe wrongly, you will confess wrongly. If you confess the wrong things, the Word will not work for you and, therefore, you will live in defeat. Some of these wrong beliefs are taught from one generation to the other, among believers. The Lord Jesus was rebuking the Pharisees and the Scribes over their hypocrisy, in **Mark 7**, and He made a very important statement:

> *Howbeit in vain do they worship me, teaching for doctrines the commandments of men... Making the word of God of none effect through your tradition, which ye have delivered: and many such like things do ye.*
> *Mark 7:7, 13 KJV*

Just like the Pharisees and the Scribes, we also fall in the same trap of creating traditions and teaching them as Bible truths. Jesus said that when we do this, we make the Word of God have no effect. No wonder we do not see the manifestation, of the presence of God, when we preach. One of the reasons for this, is that we are preaching and believing a twisted gospel – traditions of men that have been passed on, from one person to the other, and they have become accepted in the church. Many of us preachers have been guilty of misrepresenting the Lord Jesus. May we always yield to the Holy Spirit, so that we can preach the Lord Jesus as He is. Some preachers preach Christ as they want Him to be. God is the I AM, WHO I AM. He is not the, *"I AM who I want Him to be,"* like some preachers say. You cannot make God whatever you want Him to be. God is set in His ways and it is our responsibility to find out who He is. When we know who He is and approach Him as such, only then will see the answer to our petition. Faith begins where the will of God is known. If you are groping in the dark, not knowing who God is, what His Word says about things, and what your rights and privileges are in the Lord Jesus, then you are in for a defeated life. With this lack of knowledge, you are bound to accuse God of wrong doing.

God confirms His word and not traditions. So, if we believe wrong, we will not get what God has promised in the Word.

CHAPTER 2

If we teach traditions, our hearers will not be blessed and will not experience the victory that comes with the Word of God.

It the responsibility of every believer to spend time in the Word of God; to check every doctrine and every tradition that believers have adopted and see its accuracy in the light of God's Word.

The Bible speaks about a blessed man in the Epistle of James.

> *But whoso looketh into the perfect law of liberty, and continueth therein, he being not a forgetful hearer, but a doer of the work, this man shall be blessed in his deed.*
> *James 1:25 KJV*

It is our responsibility to look in the perfect law of liberty – the Word of God – and not just look once but to continue in it, and to ensure that we have an accurate understanding of what the Word says. The Bible says that when we do this, we shall be blessed. We must make up our minds to obey every command that the Lord Jesus has given us in His Word. On the other hand, we must expect the Lord Jesus to do what He said He would do in His Word.

It is also our responsibility to confirm every teaching and every *buzz phrase* that emerges, among believers, with the Word of God. This is what the believers in Berea did, when they heard Paul preach. They searched the Scriptures daily, to see if what Paul was preaching was in line with the scriptures.

> **And the brethren immediately sent away Paul and Silas by night unto Berea: who coming thither went into the synagogue of the Jews. These were more noble than those in Thessalonica, in that they received the word with all readiness of mind, and searched the scriptures daily, whether those things were so.**
> **Acts 17:10-11**

It is the responsibility of every believer to get into the Word of God and know it for themselves. If a church, which you belong to, is not teaching you what is written in the Bible, you have the right to leave it and find another one. The responsibility of the teachers and preachers is to rightly divide the Word of God. If they are adding to it or subtracting from it, you need to run away from then. If you stay, you will find yourself confessing the unbelief that you are being taught and this will bring defeat to your Christian life.

CHAPTER 2

Christianity is often called the Great Confession. This comes from the following scriptures:

> *For this reason, holy brothers, called to be partakers of a heavenly calling, consider the Apostle and High Priest of our confession, Christ Jesus...*
> *Hebrews 3:1 LITV*

> *Then having a great High Priest who has passed through the heavens, Jesus the Son of God, let us hold fast the confession.*
> *Hebrews 4:14 LITV*

If satan wants to defeat you, he will want to twist your confession; he will get it out of line with God's Word into being some manmade statements. With that, the enemy will ensure that you will never succeed in your Christian life and you will never become a threat to him. Satan knows that we overcome him by the Word of our testimony (**Revelations 12:11**). The Word of our testimony is the word that we believe and confess. When the word we believe becomes a part of us, it becomes our world view. The testimony that overcomes satan is the manner of life that you adopt, according to the Word of God. It drives you to explain life and tell stories unconsciously, according to the Word of

God, which you have believed – this is the word of your life's testimony. This must be in accordance with the written Word of God. If it is, your life will be a continuous victory over satan. We must do everything that we can, to study and cross-reference the Word for ourselves, to ensure that we believe right and therefore testify right.

The following chapters are here to correct some common statements and phrases that a number of believers have adopted and are using too frequently. These statements have become traditions and have hindered so many believers from receiving God's best.

GOD DOES NOT BRING CALAMITY?

Those people who hold the view that God will bring calamities and diseases on people, usually have their basis on the Old Testament. Here is one such scripture:

> ***And said, If thou wilt diligently hearken to the voice of the LORD thy God, and wilt do that which is right in his sight, and wilt give ear to***

> *his commandments, and keep all his statutes, I will put none of these diseases upon thee, which I have brought upon the Egyptians: for I am the LORD that healeth thee.*
> *Exodus 15:26 KJV*

The phrase that brings contention is, *"...I will put none of these diseases upon thee..."* It is written as if God was the One who brought the diseases and plagues, of Egypt, upon the Egyptians. It is this piece of Scripture and many other pieces of Scripture that the Bible Translators had translated using the *causative* sense, rather than the *permissive* sense. This is what Rev. Kenneth E. Hagin said about this, in his book, *Redeemed from Sickness, Poverty and Spiritual Death*.

> *Dr. Robert Young, author of Hints to Bible Interpretation, points out that in the original Hebrew, the verb is in the permissive rather than the causative sense. Actually, it should have been translated something like this: "The Lord will allow you to be smitten... The Lord will allow these plagues to be brought upon you..."*[2]

---

2 Hagin, Kenneth E. Redeemed from Poverty, Sickness, and Spiritual Death (Tulsa, OK: Rhema Bible Church, 1983), p. 12

Every instance, of God being responsible for bringing of evil, was in the *permissive* sense, rather than the *causative* sense. Satan is the author of evil. The Lord Jesus made this clear when He walked the face of the Earth (**Matthew 12:25-29, Luke 9:56, Luke 13:16, John 8:44, John 10:10**). Satan is the enemy of mankind. He hates man with such hatred that he is always looking to steal, kill and destroy. This guy does not take a break from pursuing the downfall of man. When given a chance, he will inflict man with all types of plagues and wickedness. However, God stops him from causing the destruction that he wants to do against mankind because God holds all things by His Word (**Hebrews 1:3**). The moments where God removed His protection, the enemy struck with calamity; these moments were translated as if God was the One Who brought the calamity on His people.

When people became disobedient to God, God then allowed the evil that satan was intending to bring on them, to overtake them (**Ecclesiastes 10:8**). In the case of Pharaoh of Egypt, it was God who kept disaster away from the Egyptians and He only allowed satan to bring the specific plagues that befell Egypt. God only allowed the angel of death to enter the homes of the people who did not have the blood of a lamb on their doorposts. It was the angel of death

– satan – who killed the firstborns of the Egyptians and not God.

The Bible says:

> ***This then is the message which we have heard of him, and declare unto you, that God is light, and in him is no darkness at all.***
> ***1 John 1:5 KJV***

One way to check if something has come from God, is to ask yourself whether or not it is part of darkness or part of the light. The Lord Jesus delivered us from the power of darkness. Everything that belongs to darkness, shall not be found in the Kingdom of the Lord Jesus. Everything that belongs to God, is permanent and will not be done away with. Everything that belongs to satan will be destroyed and done away with.

Do you see the confusion when it comes to someone who is involved in an accident and they die? Peace is disturbed; and God is not an Author of confusion but of peace (**1 Corinthians 14:33**).

Let us shift to the discipline of the Lord. The Strong's Concordance defines the word *chastisement* (discipline) as:

- to *train* up a child, that is, *educate*, or (by implication) *discipline* (by punishment): - chasten (-ise), instruct, learn, teach.

When we understand discipline, based on the explanation given above, we will begin to know how God the Father disciplines His children. He trains, educates, instructs and teaches. Some of this training can be tough but it will not damage you or kill you.

The image of God being a Father Who is punitive, always waiting to hit you on your head and inflict physical pain on you, is not correct. God has left us to deal with our physical body, to get it into alignment so that it will do what we want it to do. That is what Paul said:

> **I harden my body with blows and bring it under complete control, to keep myself from being disqualified after having called others to the contest.**
> **1 Corinthians 9:27 GNB**

The responsibility, to discipline our bodies, is ours to do. We must keep it under control. You may decide to hit your body with fasting or with physical exercise. The Psalmist said, *"I chastened my soul with fasting"* (**Psalm 69:10**). In **1**

Timothy 4:8, Paul tells Timothy that bodily exercise profits little. These two physical interventions are the best remedies for an undisciplined body. They help in bringing the body into alignment. If oversleeping is a problem that you have, that prevents you from spending time in prayer, God will not take away your bed to discipline you. Like Paul, you must do something to your body, yourself. I remember one woman of God who testified about her continuous dosing off to sleep, when she woke up to pray. She said that she would go into the bathroom and sit on the edge of the bathtub, in order to give herself a fright when she thought about the possibility of falling into the bathtub. I would not do this, but this lady said it worked for her. The measures that have a training part to them are the most effective means of disciplining the body.

When the Apostle Paul spoke about a thorn in his flesh (2 Corinthians 12:7). He did not call it a messenger of God. It was a messenger of satan. This thorn in Paul's body troubled him to keep him from being arrogant. God is not responsible for bringing persecution on His people.

Other times, we become disobedient by committing spiritual sins. We would need to be disciplined by God for this type of disobedience as well. Physical pain is not the answer for these spiritual problems; they must be dealt with by spiritual means. What methods does God use to train us and educate us? One of them is Scripture. The very Word of God. The words of God have power to transform a person's life. It is words of salvation that transformed us from sinners to saints. They transformed Cornelius, a devout Gentile man, and his household from sinners to saints (**Acts 11:14**). If they can transform a sinner, then they can correct a child of God. Let us look at how He chastised the church in Laodicea:

> *And to the angel of the assembly of Laodicea, write: These things says the Amen, the faithful and true Witness, the Head of the creation of God: I know your works, that you are neither cold nor hot. I would that you were cold, or hot. So, because you are lukewarm, and neither cold nor hot, I am about to vomit you out of My mouth. Because you say, I am rich, and I am made rich, and I have need of nothing, and do not know that you are wretched and miserable and poor and blind and naked. I advise you to buy from Me gold having been fired by fire, that you may be rich; and white garments, that you may be clothed, and your shame and nakedness may not be revealed. And anoint your eyes with eye salve, that you may see. I, as many "as I*

> *love, I rebuke and I chasten." Be zealous, then, and repent.*
> **Revelations 3:14-19 MKJV**

God gave the Laodiceans words, as His rebuke; and that rebuke was His discipline. The Word of God is capable of delivering the relevant conviction, upon a disobedient child of God, and if we are willing, it is strong enough to bring us back into line.

Paul tells Timothy that:

> *All scripture is given by inspiration of God, and is profitable for doctrine, for reproof, for correction, for instruction in righteousness: That the man of God may be perfect, thoroughly furnished unto all good works.*
> **2 Timothy 3:16-17 KJV**

Correction is the same as discipline. We see here that the Word of God, or Scripture, is capable of delivering the required disciplinary actions on us, which are necessary for us to get into alignment with God. So, what does God do to us? He speaks to you. He will speak to your spirit, which is the most common method of His communication to us. He will also speak through other people.

> *For the word of God is quick, and powerful, and sharper than any two-edged sword, piercing even to the dividing asunder of soul and spirit, and of the joints and marrow, and is a discerner of the thoughts and intents of the heart.*
> *Hebrews 4:12 KJV*

The Word of God is capable of piercing into the core of your very being, to get your attention to repent.

God will not use satanic means to discipline His children. Let us look at what the Lord Jesus said in the Gospel of Matthew:

> *If ye then, being evil, know how to give good gifts unto your children, how much more shall your Father which is in heaven give good things to them that ask him?*
> *Matthew 7:11*

The Lord Jesus compares our Heavenly Father to earthly fathers' conduct towards their children. He talks about the Heavenly Father's ability to give us good gifts. The same can be said about His ability to discipline us. If our earthly fathers can never want any satanic activities, such as sickness and disease, to come upon us, no matter how rebellious we are, how much more would the Heavenly Father? God is a better Father than we are, and He desires much better things for us than what our earthly parents do. God will not use sickness, disease, poverty, accidents and any other such satanic initiated actions in order to discipline His Children.

> *The LORD is my shepherd; I shall not want. Yea, though I walk through the valley of the shadow of death, I will fear no evil: for thou art with me; thy rod and thy staff they comfort me. Psalm 23:1, 4*

Notice that the role of the Shepherd is to provide for the sheep. We are His sheep. His obligation to provide for us, stands independent of what we do. The Lord is still the Shepherd and the Provider for the sheep that go astray, as much as He is for the obedient ones. With His staff, He rules and guides the flock to their green pastures and defends them from their enemies. With it, He also corrects them when they are disobedient and brings them back when they wander away.

God will not bring sickness and disease upon you, in order to discipline you for anything you have done. It does not matter where you have been and what you have done.

Sickness comes from the devil and God will not use it to discipline you. If you are living in sin, then you become an easier target for satan to attack; satan will afflict you with sickness. The moment you realise that it is satan who is attacking, you need to come at him with the Word of God, in the Name of the Lord Jesus. Repent and resist him strongly in the faith; and he must flee.

The Bible calls sickness an oppression of the Devil – *"...and the Lord Jesus went about healing all who were oppressed by the Devil."*

> **How God anointed Jesus of Nazareth with the Holy Spirit and with power, and He went about doing good, and healing all those who were oppressed by the Devil, for God was with Him.**
> **Acts 10:38 MKJV**

The Lord Jesus also talked about the woman, in Luke 13, who had been afflicted and was bent over, that she was bound by satan:

> **And ought not this woman, being a daughter of Abraham whom Satan has bound, lo these eighteen years, be loosened from this bond on the Sabbath day?**
> **Luke 13:16 KJV**

There are a few things that we can learn from the above Scripture:

- This sickness was caused by a spirit of infirmity
- Satan is the oppressor
- The Lord Jesus is the Deliverer

It confirms what the Apostle John wrote about in his Epistle:

> ***The one practicing sin is of the devil, because the devil sins from the beginning. For this the Son of God was revealed, that He might undo the works of the devil.***
> ***1 Johan 3:8 LITV***

Satan bound the woman; Jesus loosened her. This woman, in Luke 13, was a sinner and she must have been involved in things that were terrible. Remember, at this time, the Lord Jesus had not yet died and risen from the dead. So, there was no one who was born-again, and every person was under sin. The disease she had could have resulted from her disobedience or merely because of the fallen nature that we all find ourselves in. Whatever the case, this lady was a sinner. Jesus did not say that it was because she was sinful and that is why God brought the sickness on her. Instead, He made it clear that she was oppressed by the devil.

You need to realise that every form of sickness or disease is from the devil. You have to know this, so that you can stand in faith, against satan, to get your victory.

GOD IS NOT ALWAYS IN CONTROL

When we hold God as the One responsible, and in control, of everything that happens on planet Earth, we lose our resolve to persevere in prayer over unwanted issues in our lives. A lot of believers like making the statement, *"God is in control,"* and, yet, they do not realise that the statement is not true in every situation. Here is how it goes: whenever there is a calamity that happens to people, some preachers rise up in order to assure their hearers that God is in control of every situation.

As I am writing this book, the world has been brought to a standstill by a pandemic called COVID-19 or the Corona Virus. We have not been able to congregate, as a church, from 26 March 2020 and I am writing this on 17 May 2020. People are dying everywhere around the world and death statistics are being announced every day. Domestic violence has also increased substantially. A lot of churches are struggling to stay afloat because their members have no income and, therefore, they are not giving towards the work of God. A preacher once stood up and talked about the number of fulltime people employed in the ministry and pleaded with the hearers not to stop giving, as he did not want to retrench anyone of them. If God is in control of this situation globally then He really has made a mess of it. But friends, God is only in control to the extent that we will allow Him to be.

The famous preacher of old, John Wesley, once said, *"It seems that God is limited by our prayer life – that He can do nothing for humanity, unless someone asks Him."* When you study the Scriptures, you will find that this statement is true. The Lord Jesus, in what is called *The Lord's Prayer,* told His disciples to pray that the will of God be done on Earth. He also said we must ask God to send labourers into His field. From a natural perspective, you would almost expect that if God wants something done, He would just go ahead and do it. But this is not the case. God wants us to pray and ask Him to do things, that are His will, here on Earth. When we do not pray, or pray things that are not His will, then things that He is not in control of will happen.

Other things do not require God to act. They require the children of God to do something about them. Children of God must be willing to take dominion and enforce the authority, that the Lord Jesus gave them, here on Earth.

God's decree from Genesis to man still stands today. We have the dominion on the Earth. The Bible still calls satan, *"the god of this world…"* (2 Corinthians 4:4). Man handed over his dominion, on the Earth, to satan because of sin. Satan is the guy who is in control in every place that people have allowed him to be, and he still brings chaos in the world. It is satan who is in control of all the abortion clinics, which are slaughtering thousands of babies every year. He receives control through everyone who allows him by submitting themselves to his evil desires and schemes. We must arise, as children of God, and take possession of what belongs to us, by declaring and believing what the Word says about us: who we are, what belongs to us, and forbid or resist satan from every place that he is bringing havoc into. We must also call on the Lord, for Him to come to our defence. We are free moral beings who can allow either God or satan to work with us, to bring whatever we desire or unintentionally ask for (in the case of satan) to manifest in our lives.

Most of the people who cling onto the phrase, *"God is in control,"* believe that God can do whatever He wants to do in this world, independent of man. If you believe this, then you will also believe that He can do anything. Based on the omnipotent characteristic of God, this is correct. And saying the opposite sounds like you are sinning. However, you must also understand the power of God's Word that He has spoken. It is true that God is omnipotent; it is also true that there is nothing impossible with Him. But it is also true that it is impossible for God to lie. It is also impossible for God to break the Word that He has spoken. If it was possible for God to break the principles of His own Word, in order to do anything, then He would have sent a legion of angels to destroy the people who crucified the Lord Jesus. In fact, He would not have gone through the painful process, which led to our redemption. He could have just annihilated satan and gotten rid of him, and all the demons, permanently by a single blow and then rescued us. He could have said, *"Let bygones be bygones. You are My creation. I have forgiven you. Let us start all over now that Satan is no more."* There would be no more temptation and no more sin. But no, He did not do that. Instead, He had to follow His own Word, by fulfilling the demands of justice set by His own Word. God cannot just do anything that is outside the principles of His Word. He has to remain just before men, demons and angels.

God gave dominion over the Earth to Adam. But when Adam sinned, he legally passed this dominion over to satan. You will see satan confirming this when he was tempting Jesus.

> *And the devil, taking him up into an high mountain, shewed unto him all the kingdoms of the world in a moment of time. And the devil said unto him, All this power will I give thee, and the glory of them: for that is delivered unto me; and to whomsoever I will I give it. If thou therefore wilt worship me, all shall be thine. And Jesus answered and said unto him, Get thee behind me, Satan: for it is written, Thou shalt worship the Lord thy God, and him only shalt thou serve.*
> **Luke 4:5-8 KJV**

Satan said that all the power and the glory, of the kingdoms of this world, was delivered to him. Who delivered it to satan? God gave it to Adam and Eve. It was Adam who delivered it to satan. We know that what satan said, to the Lord Jesus, is true because the Lord Jesus did not dispute that claim; and secondly, if satan's claim was false then the Lord Jesus would have known, and it could not have been a temptation at all. If the writers of the New Testament wrote a lie and called it a temptation then they, together with the Bible, could have been a fraud. But thank God they are not! So, satan's claim to having power, over the kingdoms of this world, was legitimate. He indeed is the god of this world.

In addition to the above Scripture, in Luke, the Holy Spirit inspired the Apostle Paul to call satan the god of this world:

> *But if our gospel be hid, it is hid to them that are lost: In whom the god of this world hath blinded the minds of them which believe not, lest the light of the glorious gospel of Christ, who is the image of God, should shine unto them.*
> *2 Corinthians 4:3-4 KJV*

So, satan, being the god of this world, is working through and through with the many evil men and women everywhere, to bring havoc onto this Earth. When evil people are in control of the economic sector, they withhold resources, so that people who need them cannot benefit from them. If they are in government, they make ungodly laws to kill children before they are born; to allow wickedness to thrive in the nation. And in the meantime, their *god* - who is the thief, killer and destroyer – unleashes his character onto them.

These savage attacks will sometimes affect us, as children of God, but the Bible has given us tools to overcome satan:

- By the blood of the Lamb and the word of our testimony (Revelations 12:11);

- By our faith (1 John 5:4);

- By resisting satan and he flees from us (James 4:7, 1 Peter 5:9); and

- By prayer, asking God to help us and scatter our enemies (Psalm 68:1).

In Matthew 10:1, the Lord Jesus gave us power to drive out evil spirits. These evil spirits are inside people and these people are capable of doing terrible things. But through God, we have the power over these evil spirits that control them. Let us exercise this power, in the Name of the Lord Jesus, and drive out these evil spirits.

When we enforce the Word of God, against every circumstance that satan brings against us, we can then rest assured that God will take control of every situation. This is why the Bible says, *"All things work together for good (not to everyone) but to those who love the Lord and are the called according to His purpose"* (Romans 8:28). As believers, we must learn to cast all our cares, worries, anxieties and concerns on the Lord Jesus because He cares for us (1 Peter 5:7). We must pray to the Lord and ask Him for help. Prayer gives God permission to intervene in the affairs of men. If we do not pray, we are saying that we are able to handle matters on our own. Of course, there are some matters that we can handle on our own and this is because God gives us strength. However, when an issue becomes a care, worry or anxiety, then we must be quick to get onto our knees to ask for help.

I do not need to ask God for bread because I have money to buy bread, however, I will thank Him for the provision of bread. If I need something that I do not have, then I will need to bring it before God in prayer. Once we hand it over to Him, we must leave it there and let Him deal with it. He is able to keep what has been committed to Him (2 Timothy 1:12). What remains is thanksgiving and speaking of those things that be not as though they were (Romans 4:17).

So, if satan has done something that seems to be weighing you down with worry, cast it on the Lord Jesus. God cannot resolve the issue for you if you keep holding on to it through worry. Notice here that the Bible says, *"Cast."* When you cast something, you do not hand it over gently; you throw it. You throw it on the Lord, like you would a hot piece of coal into a safe direction and without hesitation. If you found yourself holding a hot piece of coal, you would not take your time in holding onto it because it would certainly burn your hand. You immediately throw it away. That is how you deal with cares and worries. The longer they stay with your, the more damage they do to your wellbeing. Holding onto cares and worries is not doing things in faith; and everything that is not done in faith, is sin (Romans 14:23). Modern-day Christians know that worry is a sin, so they would rather say, *"I am concerned."* Well, that also needs to be cast onto the Lord. Commit it to Him and stop worrying. Worrying makes you play into the hands of satan. You step out of the faith-realm, where you have victory, and into the fleshly-realm, where satan is god. You can never get the victory in that realm because satan is calling the shots there.

All authority in Heaven and on Earth was given to the Lord Jesus. He then delegated that authority to His Church. The Lord Jesus is in control, in this world, only through the conquest of His body (the Church). Being given authority is one thing, while enforcing the authority given is another. There are many people who have been given authority, but they do not exercise this authority and, therefore, the areas in their control are controlled by opposite forces.

Authority does not automatically eliminate any wrong behaviour done by the bad guys. Police Officers have authority in the countries where they live. However, this authority does not stop the activities of thieves and robbers, unless these thieves and robbers have been arrested and placed behind bars. In some crime ridden areas, there are some Police Officers who go about driving around and watching criminals dealing in criminal activities. Some Police Officers do not even want to go into some of these places to patrol. Drug lords are in charge of these streets because the law enforcement people are busy sleeping. In some instances, these law enforcement people are criminals themselves. Instead of enforcing the letter of the law, they participate with the criminals in doing crime. Do you think that criminals would take these types of authorities seriously? If these types of Police Officers suddenly decide that they will arrest one of his criminal friends, they would just laugh at him.

It is the same in spiritual matters. We, as believers, must know that we must go out and preach the Gospel of the Lord Jesus and enforce His victory over the kingdom of darkness. When we start to see whole suburbs, villages, towns and cities come to the saving knowledge of our Lord Jesus Christ, we will be able to see the kingdoms of this world become the kingdoms of our God and His Christ. Only then can we boldly declare that God is in total control. If we become part of the works of darkness, in one way or another, we then lose our effectiveness in enforcing the authority of the kingdom of God.

But alas, most of us are like these Police Officers who have been given the power to stop the works of darkness, in our streets, but we are not going out in order to do so. We must go out and preach the Gospel of the Lord Jesus to the people in darkness. We are hiding behind the false comfort that God is in control. We must step up and infiltrate every sector of human activities and establish the Kingdom of God. Sometimes, I intentionally drive through these crime-ridden areas of our city, declaring the Lordship of Jesus Christ over those areas. We must call on God to move and arise on our behalf in situations where there is turmoil. The Psalmist says:

> **Let God arise, let his enemies be scattered: let them also that hate him flee before him.**
> **Psalm 68:1**

We must *let God*. If we do not let Him, He will not do anything. We must pray and ask Him to do the things that only He can do. God lives inside our bodies. He is not there to be a passenger or excess baggage. He is there to be God in us and through us. Let Him live as God inside of you. You will be able to do, through Him, things that only God can do. People will marvel and think that we are superman but let us point them to the One who is doing great things in us and give Him all the glory.

CHAPTER 2

Wrong believing in just one thing can cause a huge chain reaction of various wrong beliefs that will eventually make the Word of God have no effect in your life. Believe right and see how mightily the Word of God will work for you.

THE HOLY SPIRIT IS WITH YOU FOREVER

Misunderstanding of the presence of the Holy Spirit comes from the misunderstanding of Scripture. Not knowing Who the Holy Spirit is and His assignment to the Church in the New Testament. I also used to pray and sing, to the Father, the words of Psalm 51:11, *"...take not Thy Holy Spirit from me..."* This prayer is irrelevant in the New Testament. Let us look at what the Lord Jesus says:

> *If ye love me, keep my commandments. And I will pray the Father, and he shall give you another Comforter, that he may abide with you for ever...*
> *John 14:15-16*

The Lord Jesus says that the Comforter, the Holy Spirit, will abide with us forever. He did not say that the Comforter will abide with you until you grieve Him, and then He will lift off from you like a little bird; or until you sin, and then He will leave and wait for you to repent. No, He said, the Comforter will be with us forever. Whether we are walking right or we have fallen into sin, He is always there. Of course, we grieve Him when we fall into sin, as the Bible says:

> ***And grieve not the holy Spirit of God, whereby ye are sealed unto the day of redemption.***
> ***Ephesians 4:30***

So, if we sin, we do grieve Him, but He does not leave. He is always there, and He will never leave you nor forsake you. Praise His holy Name!

> ***Without covetousness the behaviour, being content with the things present, for He hath said, 'No, I will not leave, no, nor forsake thee,'...***
> ***Hebrews 13:5 YLT***

Notice the double, *"No"* in this Young's Literal Translation. It is similar to when the Lord Jesus says, *"Verily, verily."* He is making emphasis of a point. Here, God is making a double emphasis: *"No, I will not leave, no..."* You cannot be more reassuring than that. God will not leave you. He is always there. He is always waiting on us, to turn to Him in faith, call upon Him and believe that He is doing great things in our lives, for His glory. He is the One who opens the eyes of our understanding.

When you are praying for a loved one, who has backslidden, you can ask the Holy Spirit, Who is there with them, to open their eyes, so that they may see their wrong doing and come back to God in repentance.

Another reason why this tradition has been successfully taught to us, is because we compare the Holy Spirit to a bird (the dove). This is because the Holy Spirit appeared as a dove on the Lord Jesus, as He was getting out of the waters of baptism, but it does not mean that He, Himself, is a dove. No, He is not a dove. Many people have studied the characteristics and temperaments of a dove and have translated them into the character of the Holy Spirit. Well, that is wrong. The fact that He appeared in the form of a dove, does not make Him a dove. He is God – in all His splendour, authority, power and majesty. It is true that doves do not like strife and when disturbed, they will leave and go somewhere else, where there is peace. But that is not true of God, the Holy Spirit. He does not leave just because you are arguing with your wife or husband. In fact, He sticks around to bring peace. The word that is translated as *Comforter*, in the verse we read from John 14 above, is also translated as *Standby*, in the Amplified version of the Bible. He stands by you, all the time and every time. He is not a fair-weather friend who only sticks around when things are going well with you. He is always there.

This reminds me of an old song that we used to sing at Scripture Union at Hillcrest Secondary School in Zambia:

> **He's always there when things go wrong**
> **He's always there when my hope is gone**
> **He lifts me up when am in pray'r**
> **He's never gone when I am alone**
> **He's always there**

Well, thank God for the Holy Spirit, Who is always there to help us in our infirmities (Romans 8:26).

The Holy Spirit has also appeared in the form of a flaming fire. To attribute the characteristics of a dove, to the Holy Spirit, would also imply that we attribute the characteristics of a flame to the Holy Spirit. The Holy Spirit fire is the kind of fire that Moses saw in the burning bush. The bush was engulfed with flames, but the bush was not burnt. It is also the fire that fell on the first believers in the Upper Room. It landed on each one's head, but they did not burn. The effect of this fire is what the Lord Jesus said, *"... we receive power and become His witnesses"* (Acts 1:8). This fire will not burn you out. It will give you power to serve God.

Some people go to another extreme by calling Holy Ghost fire onto their enemies. The Holy Spirit does not burn people up. He convicts the world of sin (John 16:8). This is the same world that God loved and gave His only Son to die for. Your prayer should, therefore, be that the Holy Spirit convicts the people who are working against you, so that they can turn to the Lord Jesus and be saved. Do not pray that they be struck by Holy Ghost fire. This is witchcraft. If you start following that line of thought, you will start treading into the kingdom of darkness and open yourself to demonic influence.

How did the Lord Jesus say that we should deal with our enemies? Look at Matthew 5:44 and you will find the answer.

> ***...but I—I say to you, Love your enemies, bless those cursing you, do good to those hating you, and pray for those accusing you falsely, and persecuting you...***
> ***Matthew 5:44 YLT***

You must love your enemies and bless those who curse you. So, the witch who is cursing you and casting spells on you, you must bless. Do not call fire, to come down from Heaven, to burn them up. *Loving* and *blessing* are the ways to victory.

If we continue thinking that the Holy Spirit is a dove, then we will fail to realise that He is the Almighty God Who raises the standard against the devil (Isaiah 59:19). He is the One Who dwells within us, brings wholeness to our bodies and quickens our bodies when we feel weak or frail (Romans 8:11). So, let us change our thinking with regards to Who the Holy Spirit is and His work on the Earth. Know that He is God Almighty, the Creator of the Heavens and the Earth.

He is an ever-present help in times of trouble, and He is only a prayer away. He will be there in your weakest and in your strongest point. You get baptised in the Holy Spirit once and you are permanently ready to do the work of the ministry.

The main thing that the Lord Jesus wants us to do, is to be witnesses. We must preach the Gospel to every person who we have an opportunity to come into contact with. It is for this reason that you are anointed with the Holy Spirit.

Make use of every opportunity that comes your way. The Lord Jesus said to His disciples, *"Go into ALL the world and preach the Gospel."* To preach, is to proclaim in a way that people hear and understand. One of satan's biggest deceptions is to tell believers to not preach wherever they are but, rather, live an exemplary life. We are made to feel that we should not force the Gospel onto an unbeliever in the workplace but to just live holy lives, so that it will attract the unbeliever to God. Someone coined a phrase. *"Preach the gospel and if possible, use a few words."* This is a lie, and I will tell you why. When the angel told Cornelius, in the book of Acts, to call for Peter, he did not say that this Peter would come and demonstrate how to live the Christian life. He said Peter will tell you *words* by which you will be saved (Acts 11:14). People are saved by hearing words and not by *seeing* how others live life. You must preach the Gospel, so that people will hear it. Faith for salvation will only come by hearing the Word of God (Romans 10:17). So, be bold and preach the Word. If you are timid, it is okay to pray for boldness to preach to people. The apostles did (Acts 4:17). If you have received the Holy Spirit baptism, with the evidence of speaking in tongues, then you are already anointed to preach.

Every sector of human existence is gasping for the Word of God, like a fish taken out of water gasps for water. We must preach the Word and it will bring life to those who hear it. We can occupy ourselves with our personal spiritual growth initiatives, church meetings of all sorts, prayer rallies, etc, and that is good. But, if we neglect the core purpose of seeking and saving the lost, by preaching the Word, then we have become irrelevant to the world and disobedient to the Master's command.

So, preach the Word and use plenty of Holy Spirit filled words. Peter preached to the crowd that gathered after hearing how the disciples were speaking in tongues and spoke many words:

> ***And with many other words he earnestly testified and exhorted, saying, Be saved from this perverse generation.***
> ***Acts 2:40 MKJV***

Why would we think that we can get the job done, by speaking a few words, and then think that the sinner will fill in the empty spaces by observing our lives? We must take time to preach the Word.

We must take time and preach the Word under the anointing and power of the Holy Spirit. The presence of the Holy Spirit in us is anchored on the promise of God. He said He will never leave. So, whether I feel Him or not, my trust is in the Word of God. God said He will never leave – so, I trust Him and I will go about and do what He said I must do, in His Name.

FEAR IS A SPIRIT

The force of fear is one of the greatest weapons, which satan uses to rob the people of God out of their God-given rights. One method that satan uses to get us to become accustomed to fear, is to call it a *false expectation appearing real.* This statement has no scriptural basis. It was started by motivational speakers who believed in the power of positive thinking only. Positive thinking is good, and it does help a lot. However, when it denies the existence of reality, then it does not remove the danger around it. It creates a battle in the mind, which we constantly fight; we fight the reality in our minds by convincing ourselves that it is not there, every time it raises its ugly head. The Bible has the best remedy for fear, which deals with it once and for all.

What does the Bible say about fear? The key Scripture is in 2 Timothy.

> ***For God hath not given us the spirit of fear; but of power, and of love, and of a sound mind.***
> ***2 Timothy 1:7***

From this Scripture, we learn that fear is a spirit – an evil spirit. There are other Scriptures that affirm this, and we will turn to them so that *at the mouth of two witness* this matter may be established. So, let us turn to another portion of Scripture that also talks about fear.

> ***There is no fear in love; but perfect love casteth out fear: because fear hath torment. He that feareth is not made perfect in love.***
> ***1 John 4:18***

Notice here, what the Bible says about fear. It has torment. In this sense, a person can only be tormented by a spirit. So, if fear has torment, then it is a spirit and that is why it can be cast out. There are certain situations that the devil causes around us in order to bring fear. He will, for example, cause you to lose your job and then try bringing the spirit of fear, so that it can torment you wondering how you are going to make ends meet. He did this to me when I was forced to resign from my job. I had so many commitments and debit orders going off my account. The spirit of fear came and started whispering in my ears, *"How are you going to service all of these debts that you have and pay for your children to go to school?"* I was troubled for a while over this and it did give me several sleepless nights. But when I went into a time of prayer, the Holy Spirit brought Philippians 4:19 to my remembrance, *"My God shall supply all my needs according to his riches in glory by Christ Jesus."* The Word of God says that He will supply *my needs* – not according to my employment, but according to His riches in glory.

Why does perfect love cast out fear? When I was teaching this lesson to my children, I reminded them about when they were younger; about how they enjoyed it when I tossed them into the air. I would arrive home from work and my daughter would run to me, throwing herself into my hands, so that I would through her up into the air. She always looked forward to the feeling of being airborne. Whenever any of my friends offered to do this to her, she would refuse the offer. Why would she agree to be thrown into the air by me and not by my friends? Because she was confident in my love for her. She knew I could never let her fall. The same applies to believers; if we are confident in the love of God, to take care of us, we will not be anxious when we have moments of suspense, when we have been tossed into the air and seemingly there are only two options: to fall to the ground and crash, or to be caught in the everlasting arms of our Saviour.

When fear comes, it comes to try and obscure the power of faith, in the Word, in order to stop us from being able to deal with situations that are averse to us. However, fear gets ejected when we realise that God loves us too much to leave us unaided. When we embrace the Word of God, what it says about us and the victory that we have in His Word, fear leaves. When we speak the Word of God over our situation and refuse to become fearful, that spirit will have no choice but to leave.

The notion that fear is *false expectations appearing real* takes the focus away from the Word and puts it onto self. A feeling of self-sufficiency, where we can deal with fear on our own by passively ignoring it. This attitude robs the believer of trusting the power of faith, in the Word of God, to overcome fear. David said that whenever he was afraid, he would trust in the Lord (Psalm 56:3); not in himself nor ignore the fear. Why? Because the source of fear is a real enemy – satan. He wants to steal, kill and destroy.

A lot of contradictory statements have been made about the fear that grips us when we see dangerous animals. Some writers claim that it is necessary for us to fear because we must flee. This claim has been contradicted by some other writers and researchers, saying that a fearless approach to handling these wild animals will create a situation where the animal will not feel threatened by our response and will then be less likely to attack. We must train ourselves to be calm, if we find ourselves in the midst of wild animals.

Off course, we must make our escape with urgency but fearlessly. We have been given dominion over every creation of God, therefore, I believe that you can speak to the animal, if it is showing signs of aggression against you, and command it to be calm.

In the same way, if you need to make your escape from an oncoming vehicle, that is moving towards you, you can do so with the relevant sense of urgency but fearlessly. If fear grips you, it may make you so paralysed that you fail to think of a way for escape. There is no need to fear. The chemicals that rush into your system, in a moment of danger, is a reaction where we are required to give strength to our system to respond appropriately. People who fear, in the case of an emergency, are a danger to themselves and others. When you are calm but acting with the relevant sense of urgency, you will calm the roughest storm against you.

THE BODY AND BLOOD OF THE LORD JESUS

The power of Holy Communion is another source of victory that we must take advantage of. With this, once again, we have been taught and we have embraced tradition, and to such an extent that when we take the Holy Communion, we do not expect any change in our situations. Let us look at what the Bible says:

> ***And as they were eating, Jesus took bread, and blessed it, and brake it, and gave it to the disciples, and said, Take, eat; this is my body. And he took the cup, and gave thanks, and gave it to them, saying, Drink ye all of it; For this is my blood of the new testament, which is shed for many for the remission of sins. Matthew 26:26-28***

In reference to the bread of the communion, the Lord Jesus said, *"This is my body,"* and not, *"This is a **symbol** of my body,"* like most of us say. With regards the juice we drink, the Lord Jesus again said, *"This is my blood."* I grew up knowing that we are partaking of *symbols* and not the body and the blood of the Lord Jesus. When we pray over the bread and drink of Holy Communion, we take them by faith as the body and blood of the Lord Jesus. My Pentecostal background battled with this, but I later came to learn, from the Word of God, that this is right. The bread we eat and the juice we drink, during Communion, are the body and the blood of our Lord Jesus Christ, respectively. When we realise and understand this, we will see the power of Holy

Communion. We will realise that we are eating of His body and drinking His blood. We can, therefore, claim the benefits thereof, according to what He said, as recorded by the Apostle John:

> *Then Jesus said unto them, Verily, verily, I say unto you, Except ye eat the flesh of the Son of man, and drink his blood, ye have no life in you. Whoso eateth my flesh, and drinketh my blood, hath eternal life; and I will raise him up at the last day. For my flesh is meat indeed, and my blood is drink indeed. He that eateth my flesh, and drinketh my blood, dwelleth in me, and I in him. As the living Father hath sent me, and I live by the Father: so he that eateth me, even he shall live by me. This is that bread which came down from heaven: not as your fathers did eat manna, and are dead: he that eateth of this bread shall live for ever.*
> *John 6:53-58*

When the bread and juice, of the Holy Communion, is set apart and consecrated by a word of prayer, we must receive it by faith as the body and blood of the Lord Jesus. When we eat it, we ingest the vitality of God into our bodies. The body of the Lord Jesus did not get attacked by sickness and disease and so, when we eat of the communion bread, we take in the health of the body of our Lord into our own bodies. We take of Holy Communion as frequently as possible. We can even take it on a daily basis.

The Apostle Paul realised the gravity of the bread and juice of the Holy Communion. He said to the Corinthian Church that they must not partake of the Holy Communion by eating and drinking in large quantities, like they would do at home. The Holy Communion bread must be broken off and taken in small quantities. Similarly, with the juice, it must be placed in a cup and sipped in small quantities, after having prayed over it.

The Apostle Paul further says:

> ***The cup of blessing which we bless, is it not the communion of the blood of Christ? The bread which we break, is it not the communion of the body of Christ?***
> ***1 Corinthians 10:16 KJV***

> ***Wherefore whosoever shall eat this bread, and drink this cup of the Lord, unworthily, shall be guilty of the body and blood of the Lord.***
> ***1 Corinthians 11:27 KJV***

Therefore, when you partake of the bread and the juice, during Holy Communion, you partake of the body and the blood of the Lord Jesus Christ. When you realise this, then John 6 becomes a reality. When you eat of the body of the Lord Jesus and drink His blood, you receive the very life of the Lord Jesus in you. His flesh brings you vitality and re-energises you to become a super-human, flowing with the divine life of God, Himself. You can, therefore, claim every benefit that the Lord Jesus talked about in the Gospel of John above. You can claim life, as defined in John 10:10 – life to the full, until it overflows. This is life, with no sicknesses. You can claim a rejuvenated physical body, with renewed energy and strength.

People have taken Holy Communion, in faith, and have seen their physical bodies being renewed; looking younger than they really are. This is the blessing of Holy Communion. It will reverse the aging process in you, in order to get you to do more things for the glory of God. It does not mean that we will not die. It just means that our strength will be renewed, and our bodies will function well, until the number of our days are fulfilled. Holy Communion facilitates the blessing of Abraham, of vitality, upon the believer. As we eat of the Lord's body, our bodies are energised to be like His – a strong body in its thirties. The Lord pronounced a blessing upon Abraham, which was the reversal of physical limitations that Abraham had due to age. The blessing was upon him and his wife Sarah. The blessing vitalised Sarah to such an extent that a heathen Egyptian king got attracted to her when she was sixty-five years old (Genesis 12). There were many young beautiful Egyptian girls in Egypt, but the blessing made Sarah out class each one of them and the Egyptian princes had to recommend her to Pharaoh for a wife. When the time came for Sarah to be with child, she had stopped attending to the matters of women, however, when this blessing came upon her, she was able to ovulate and conceive.

Abraham was so energised that not only was he able to get his wife Sarah to conceive, but he went ahead to marry another woman (Keturah) after the death of Sarah, and he then had more children with her, post one hundred years old. This is the kind of vitality we receive when we take of Holy Communion.

The Lord Jesus' broken body units every area of our lives, which the enemy has torn apart. Families are mended when they join themselves together at the table of the Lord and receive communion. Husband and wife are brought into harmony when they join hands and take Holy Communion together.

CHAPTER 2

When you realise the truth of receiving the benefits that Holy Communion brings, you should then do your own study of this important sacrament and take it on a regular basis. You will see the results, as the Holy Spirit reveals them to your spirit.

THE FAVOUR OF GOD IS AVAILABLE TO ALL

> *Paul, an apostle of Jesus Christ by the will of God, and Timotheus our brother, to the saints and faithful brethren in Christ which are at Colosse: Grace be unto you, and peace, from God our Father and the Lord Jesus Christ.*
> *Colossians 1:1 KJV*

The Apostle Paul says, *"Grace be unto you and peace, from God our Father and the Lord Jesus Christ."* The Literal Translation says, *"Grace and peace to you from God our Father and the Lord Jesus Christ."* Grace and Peace are received from both God, our Father, and the Lord Jesus Christ, making us understand that from the Lord Jesus Christ also proceeds Grace and Peace. This is a testimony of the Deity of the Lord Jesus Christ – He is God.

According to W.E. Vine Expository Dictionary of the New Testament[3], there are two Greek words that have been translated as *grace* in the New Testament – Charis and Euprepeia. Our focus is on Charis.

Charis – Grace is that which bestows pleasure, delight and causes **favourable regard**. It is God's redemptive mercy – the compassion of His heart towards the human race. It is free and applied universally.

The compassion of the heart of God will overlook our short comings and celebrate our most minimal effort and meet us at the point of our need, even when we have not done everything right.

It is important to understand that grace is universally applied. Too many preachers, today, are making people think that special favour can only be released by them, and to a specific individual, and that it is not available to others. Everyone has grace to do the assignment that they have been given. You do not get grace to get a great job. You get grace because you have a great job to do, or you are going through a rough patch that is necessary for your

---

3 Expository Dictionary of New Testament Words, W.E. Vine, Zondervan Publishing House, 1952

development. This, therefore, shifts the responsibility for more grace to be on the person who must work and not the one who must give grace.

A lot of believers have delegated their responsibility of working hard and put in their best, in order to gain the *favour* of God. I remember when I was in boarding school, for my undergraduate degree, we would often say, before facing a tough exam that we did not prepare for, *"This one will be by grace."* We laze around and we are not diligent in preparing ourselves for what we are required to do. Instead, we depend on *grace* to see us through. God has given us capabilities physically, intellectually and in every area of our lives. We must, therefore, use these capabilities to rise and become the best that we can be in life, and the grace of God will be there to sustain us. If you are a student, study hard; if you are an employee, work hard; if you are a politician, serve well and campaign hard; if you are a farmer, work hard and plant plenty of seed on time. There is no substitute for good old-fashioned hard work, discipline, and diligence, whenever we want to see the best results, in whatever we are doing; and we can all do it. The greater the assignment, the more effort you must put in to achieve the assignment.

Remember that the grace of God will be there to see that every effort you apply will result in something positive.

Hebrews 4:16 says that we come boldly before God, so that we may find grace to help us. Grace helps you with what you are doing and not with what you are not doing. We are co-labourers with God. We must remember to do our part and let God do His. We must intelligently, entirely and professionally apply ourselves to do the work of God and do everything the Holy Spirit is telling us to do. Grace is what sustains you when you work extra hours, more than the ordinary person. It is grace that sustains you when you sleep less hours, than what is required, because you have to achieve a certain target. You cannot leave work incomplete and give yourself half-heartedly to a course and still expect that favour will make you become the better person, amongst everyone else.

God has made grace available to everyone and this grace is free; not because of what we have done, but because of what the Lord Jesus has done.

> ***For by grace are ye saved through faith; and that not of yourselves: it is the gift of God: Not of works, lest any man should boast.***
> ***Ephesians 2:8-9 KJV***

When we yielded to the call of God, stepped forward and believed in the Lord Jesus as our Saviour, God favoured us and gave us grace to be saved. Salvation is a free gift, but we must receive it. The Father draws us to Himself, by sending a preacher to us who preaches the Word. We believe that Word and we then become saved. The favour, or grace, to be saved has been extended to every human being upon the face of the Earth.

> *For the grace of God that bringeth salvation hath appeared to all men, Teaching us that, denying ungodliness and worldly lusts, we should live soberly, righteously, and godly, in this present world...*
> *Titus 2:11-12 KJV*

Friends, every person on planet Earth has been presented with the grace that they need in order to be saved. But not everyone is saved because not everyone has cashed in on what has freely been given to them. Today, if you have not received the Lord Jesus Christ as your personal Saviour, this grace, that God has given for all people, has appeared to you. Get hold of it, believe it and receive your salvation.

> *Not by works of righteousness which we have done, but according to his mercy he saved us,*

> *by the washing of regeneration, and renewing of the Holy Ghost...*
> *Titus 3:5 KJV*

> *Therefore, it is of faith, that it might be by grace; to the end the promise might be sure to all the seed; not to that only which is of the law, but to that also which is of the faith of Abraham; who is the father of us all.*
> *Romans 4:16 KJV*

God has bestowed upon you favour not because of what you did, but because of what the Lord Jesus did through His death, burial and resurrection. It is by His own love. God's love sees past your failures and mistakes and looks at the human being, which was created in His image – He has a strong desire to restore you, to fellowship with Himself, so He gives you grace.

When you are bestowed with pleasure, you become pleasant and desirable for great things, and great people will desire your presence. We have all become favourable and have favour with the people that matter. This is what you find, in this verse here:

> *Praising God, and having favor with all the people. And the Lord added to the assembly, the*

CHAPTER 2

ones being saved from day to day.
Acts 2:47 KJV

Favour comes with responsibility; it comes with great expectations of the favoured, to use every resource they have been favoured with, to the fullest extent for the benefit of humanity. When you are obedient in executing the assignment that God has given to you, you will have favour with more and more people. More and more doors of opportunity will open for you to do greater things. There is no need to worry about success in the time of famine; you will succeed if you step out to plant in the time of famine. Success is guaranteed because the favour of God is available to you, as you work at seeing your God-given dreams come to pass, in your life for the glory of God and for the benefit of mankind.

GOD DOES NOT TAKE AWAY GOOD THINGS FROM US

There are many times when we lose good things and then blame it on God. However, the Bible says that God will not withhold any good thing from those who walk uprightly (Psalm 84:11). In the Old Testament, the uprightness of a person was judged by their own deeds. However, because

God wanted to show the extent of His extravagant love to us, He cut a New Covenant with Himself, and we are the beneficiaries of this Covenant. Instead of demanding that the other side of the Covenant be fulfilled by man in order for God to fulfil His part, both sides of the Covenant were fulfilled by God. The standard of uprightness that is required to release the goodness of God, upon mankind, is the uprightness of the Lord Jesus. God will, therefore, not hold back in being good to us because of what the Lord Jesus has already done for us. When He looks at us, He sees the righteousness of His Son, the Lord Jesus Christ, and that is sufficient for Him to continue being good to us.

James 1:17 says that every good and perfect gift comes from God. What happens then when your good and perfect gift becomes sour and bitter? There are times when a God-given spouse becomes estranged or a God-given child becomes abusive. You must turn to the One Who gave you this person and let Him sort it out for you. Never give up on your marriage, just because your spouse become estranged; rather, dig deep in yourself and find forgiveness. Forgive them and fight for your marriage. God will work with you, in order to bring them back into unity with you again.

There are some God-given gifts that we are not meant to keep permanently. To decide on this, we need to be guided by the Word of God. Marriage, for example, is for keeps – *until death do you part*. However, when there is abuse in a marriage and one spouse backslides to such an extent that they become violent and endanger the life of the other spouse, the immediate action, by the spouse in danger, must be to leave to go to a safe place. You can still work out the marriage from different places of residence but, please, do not stay in an abusive relationship.

God will give and not withhold, when we are in need of anything good. When we say that God gave to us and then He took it away, we are bringing an unfair accusation against Him. I have some preachers say this at funerals of young lives, which have been taken away premature. God is not always responsible for taking away loved ones from us. God's intention, for our lives, is that we must fulfil the number of our days – until we have finished His assignment here on Earth. Please get hold of my book *You shall live and not die*.

For now, it suffices to say that the Bible gives a promise to children, who honour their parents, that they will live long. If children die early, it is not God's intent. We must stand against the spirit of death and resist the devil in the Name of the Lord Jesus.

The statement, *"God gave, and God took away,"* was made by Job, after his children and all that he had was destroyed by satan. We know that it was satan who destroyed Job's property but then he attributed it to God. When you see the character of God, as revealed by the Lord Jesus Christ, you see that God does not take away anything good from us. He gives and gives and gives.

> *If ye then, being evil, know how to give good gifts unto your children, how much more shall your Father which is in heaven give good things to them that ask him?*
> *Matthew 7:11 KJV*

If the good that you have been given is destroyed, or taken away, know who to target your attention to – it is satan. In John 10:10, the Bible calls him a thief who comes to steal, kill and destroy.

Recently, I had to help one of my dear brothers, in the Lord, who lost his salary for the month of March 2020, due to COVID-19. As far as he was concerned, God was the One who took away his salary, so that he could now fall down at God's feet to worship Him. This is not true. Satan is the thief that came to steal.

CHAPTER 2

PRAY AND NEVER GIVE UP

We must remember that God always answers prayer. When we come before God, in prayer, and pray according to His will, we are guaranteed of the answer. God's will is His Word. So, before you pray about something, find out what His Word says concerning the matter you are praying about and come boldly before God. Sometimes, we need to find out, from the Word of God, which Scripture we are standing on and what the true intentions of our motives are, for that which we are asking God for. When you are looking for Scriptures, be sure to find it in the New Testament and not only in the Old Testament.

There are many things that the Lord Jesus did for us that have given us more than what the Old Testament saints had. When you are praying for your enemies, the Old Testament says a number of vengeful things; Psalm 35, as an example. In the New Testament, we have victory in forgiveness and seeking the good of others, no matter how badly they may have behaved towards us (Mark 11:25). We have been endowed with the capacity of the Lord Jesus to love as He loved, and to forgive as He forgives. We love as He loves. So, we live in the New Testament and everything that the Lord Jesus accomplished, through His death, burial and resurrection, is ours in Him.

Before I continue, I must first say that prayer is communication with God. I do not like to use the word *talking* for *communication* because there are certain types of prayer where we do not *talk* with God but, rather, we *communicate* with Him in groanings that cannot be uttered with words (Romans 8:26). There are many kinds of prayer that we can pray. Some of them are as follows:

1. Praise and worship – when we praise and worship God, we are communing with Him and, therefore, we are praying.

2. Studying and meditating on God's Word – reading and meditating on God's Word are sure ways through which God speaks to us and we also speak with Him, as we understand what He is saying. This too is a kind of prayer. We commune with God through His Word.

3. Petition, supplication and asking – in this prayer, we ask for things from God.

4. Intercessory prayer – when we pray for others.

When the will of God, about what we are asking for, is known, we ask once and then the rest of the time, we thank God for the answer. The Scripture that gives guidance on which kind of prayer you should pray, when you ask God for something, is in Mark 11:22-24:

> *And Jesus answering saith unto them, Have faith in God. For verily I say unto you, That whosoever shall say unto this mountain, Be thou removed, and be thou cast into the sea; and shall not doubt in his heart, but shall believe that those things which he saith shall come to pass; he shall have whatsoever he saith. Therefore I say unto you, What things soever ye desire, when ye pray, believe that ye receive them, and ye shall have them.*

When you pray about something, which you know is the will of God for you, you must believe that you have received what you have prayed for and it shall be yours. For, example, you know that it is the will of God for you to be well in your body. So, if you are praying for healing, pray once and believe that you have received and walk away from the prayer line, or your prayer room, knowing that you have received what you asked for. The will of God has been revealed to us in the Word of God – the Bible – concerning healing (1 Peter 2:24).

Satan will, almost always, bring a second and third attack onto the people who receive healing for their body.

You must stand firm in the confession of your healing. Remember that you are healed because the Word of God says so, and not because you are feeling well and pain free.

If the will of God has not been revealed in the Word of God: for example, if you are praying for sister X to be your wife, there is no scripture that says sister X will marry brother Y; you then need to pray a prayer of consecration that seeks to have the will of God, in this matter, to be done.

Christian people waste precious fellowship time, with their Father, and meditation time, in the Word, while they are in prayer because they spend too much time hopping on the same prayer item. Pray the most minimal number of words without vain repetitions. The Bible says that even before you call, your Father in Heaven will answer you. Once you have made your request know before God, what remains is a time of thanksgiving every time you remember the request. Known prayer requests should not take long. They should be thoroughly articulated to the best of your description and once you have presented them before God, leave them with Him and expect to see the results.

Prolonged prayer is essential for certain kinds of prayers. When you are having fellowship with God and you are worshiping and praising Him, you can obviously do that for as long as you want to. Here, you take your time in telling God Who He is to you and thank Him for what He has done.

You can also prolong your prayers when you are praying in other tongues, for someone else, or you are merely building yourself up. When you do intercessory prayer, there are many areas that you may need to bring before God, on behalf of someone else, and that is why you would tarry longer in prayer. When you are praying in tongues for someone who may be in danger, you may not even know who that person is and what type of danger they are in, unless the Holy Spirit shows you; otherwise you would tarry in prayer, until you sense victory in your spirit.

Jesus has elevated our status – we are now friends of God.

> *Greater love hath no man than this, that a man lay down his life for his friends. Ye are my friends, if ye do whatsoever I command you. Henceforth I call you not servants; for the servant knoweth not what his lord doeth: but I have called you friends; for all things that I have heard of my Father I have made known unto you.*
> *John 15:13-15*

We can talk to God as a man talks with his friends (Exodus 33:11). You do not hype yourself up and raise your voice, when you are talking to your friends, do you? And yet, that is what many of us do when we are praying. There is a place for a raised voice, especially when you are in public worship, so that other people can hear you and say, *"Amen,"* to your prayer. But when you are alone, there is no need to holler and scream in prayer. Your Heavenly Father hears you when you call, and the Bible says His ear is attentive to our prayers (1 Peter 3:12).

When you are going to pray, it is always a good starting point to find Scriptures that give you promises regarding the issue that you are going to pray about.

CHAPTER 3
YOU ARE PERMANENTLY IN THE LORD

The recording of the Lord's statement, in John 15:2, has brought about one anomaly. Let us look at it in the King James Version and then the Good News version of the Bible:

> *Every branch in me that beareth not fruit he taketh away: and every branch that beareth fruit, he purgeth it, that it may bring forth more fruit.*
> *John 15:2 KJV*

> *He breaks off every branch in me that does not bear fruit, and he prunes every branch that does bear fruit, so that it will be clean and bear more fruit.*
> *John 15:2 GNV*

When you read this verse, in the Good News Version of the Bible, you are left with the impression that the Father is responsible for breaking off those of His children who do not bear fruit. The King James Version is not clear when it says *He taketh away*. Where does He take the branch to? Strong's Dictionary has the following to say about the phrase *taketh away*:

It comes from the Greek word - **ah'ee-ro**: a primary verb; to *lift*; by implication to *take up* or *away*. So, this Scripture could also have been translated as – *Every branch in Me that beareth not fruit He lifts (or takes up)*. This interpretation is more aligned with the character of the Father and the Lord Jesus. He lifts up every branch IN HIM that does not bear fruit. He lifts you up, so that you can be exposed to the life-giving Word. He brings you to a place where you are raised above the things that would want to drown your faith and exposes you to the brilliance of His glory. What fruit are we required to bear, as children of God? There are a lot of different types of fruit that we bear; part of some of them are found in Galatians 5: 22-23:

> *But the fruit of the Spirit is love, joy, peace, longsuffering, gentleness, goodness, faith, Meekness, temperance: against such there is no law.*
> ***Galatians 5:22-23***

We are to bear the fruit of love, joy, peace, etc. There are seasons in life where we do not respond appropriately to people and we do not bear the love fruit. Would the Father break us off from the Lord Jesus? If He would, many of us would have been broken off. I have heard of Christians becoming depressed. Depression is the absence of joy and peace. When you are depressed, you are not bearing the joy and peace fruit. Again, would the Father break you off from the Lord Jesus? The answer is, *"No. He would not."*

The Bible says that the Lord Jesus will not break a bruised reed nor will He quench a smoking flax (Matthew 12:20); and the Father heals the broken hearted and binds up their wounds (Psalm 147:3). When you are not on the cutting edge of your relationship with God, in the place where you are not bearing fruit, you have a Friend that will stick closer to you than a brother would – His name is Jesus. The Bible says that He lives to make intercession for you and me.

The difference between the treatment that the Lord gives a fruit bearing believer and the believer who does not bear fruit is interesting. The believer, who does not bear fruit, is lifted so that he can be exposed to a higher life, just like a branch is lifted to be exposed to sunlight. I am reminded of the story of the lost sheep, where the owner of the sheep leaves the ninety-nine sheep to go after the one lost sheep; and when he finds it, he lifts it up and lays it on his shoulders (Luke 15:5). This is the treatment, of a believer who does not bear fruit, from the Lord. Satan wants to place guilt on you, especially if you had backslidden before and you are trusting God for healing or receiving something from Him. The devil says to you, *"You have not been bearing fruit, so you have been broken off the main vine."* You must resist him, in the Name of the Lord Jesus, and he will flee from you. Of course, you cannot continue to live a life of sin and expect that you will have all the blessings that God has to offer. You must repent and turn away from your wicked ways. If you continue in sin, you are placing yourself in the direct line of attack of satan; and be warned, he will strike.

The concept that the Father removes those believers, who do not bear fruit, from the Body of Christ, is not consistent with the Fatherhood of God. The Lord Jesus portrays God the Father as a loving Father Who is always looking out for the good of His children. He is doing His very best to keep them in His family. The Lord Jesus said that the Father, in whose hands we are, is greater than all. No one can snatch you out of His hands. When you read the story of the prodigal son, who left home with his portion of the inheritance, the father was looking out for his son every day. It was the father who first saw the son coming because he was looking forward to having him back. The Father did not say, of the prodigal son, *"... since this son of mine is not fruitful to me – he is not tending the livestock and contributing to the welfare of the family – I will cut ties with him and cut him off from my family."* He did not do that. He longed to have him restored to the family and when the youngman arrived, he was treated to a stately banquet. That is the Father's love for all of His children.

In the Old Testament, God the Father was giving an invitation to backslidden Israel when He said:

> ***Come now, and let us reason together, saith the LORD: though your sins be as scarlet, they shall be as white as snow; though they be red like crimson, they shall be as wool.***
> ***Isaiah 1:18***

God wants to have a relationship with us permanently. There are things that may distract us from Him, however, God always has a plan of getting us out of them and into a solid relationship with Him. God does not cast anyone away, even if we have sinned. His arms are open wide towards us, so that we can return to Him, repent and He will forgive, forget and treat us as if we never did anything bad.

> ***For we have not an high priest which cannot be touched with the feeling of our infirmities;***

> *but was in all points tempted like as we are, yet without sin. Let us therefore come boldly unto the throne of grace, that we may obtain mercy, and find grace to help in time of need.*
> **Hebrews 4:15-16**

The Bible encourages us to come boldly before the presence of God, despite our weaknesses and infirmities. It is during the times of weaknesses that we must become even bolder in approaching the Throne of Grace. Do not try to resolve that matter alone. Step forward to the Throne of God and God will help you. He will strengthen you. Grace is for those who need help. So, if you are in a place of weakness, sin or fruitlessness, come boldly before the Throne of Grace because you will find grace to help you in your area of need. Praise the Lord.

CHAPTER 4

VICTORY BELONGS TO YOU IN THE LORD JESUS

Let us start this teaching by referring to a relevant Scripture about victory:

> ***But thanks be to God, which giveth us the victory through our Lord Jesus Christ.***
> ***1 Corinthians 15:57***

Most of us have no problem ascribing victory to the Lord Jesus. But we hold back in emphatically declaring that we, as children of the Living God, also have victory. Now, this is very disturbing. It is typical for a lot of believers to only ascribe certain characteristics to the Lord Jesus and yet, those same characteristics belong to the church and to individual believers as well. Victory, indeed, belongs to us. It belongs to you and me. You have victory over everything that the Lord Jesus overcame when He died, rose from the dead and sat at the right hand of the Father. Everything

Jesus did, He did it for His body – the church, of which you are part of, if you have received Him as your Lord and Saviour.

Let us look at some of the Scriptures that talk about this:

> *"... we are more than conquerors..."*
> **Romans 8:37**

A conqueror is a person who goes out to fight in a battle and conquers the enemy. The Bible does not say that we are conquerors – it says we are **more** than conquerors. The Lord Jesus has overcome, on our behalf, and we merely come behind Him and walk in a triumphant procession to reinforce the victory. God the Father causes us to triumph in Christ Jesus, our Lord (2 Corinthians 2:14), as we walk in faith and believe that everything in our lives will turn out exactly according to what the Word says. In other words, it shall be to you exactly according to what the Word says (1 John 5:4). With that attitude in life, you cannot be defeated by anything.

So, the Lord Jesus gives us victory over all things. Notice here, the Scripture says, *"God gives us the victory."* He does not lend it to us for short period of time and then take it back for whatever reason – no. He gives it to us as our personal possession. We have victory, given to us by God the Father, in the Name of the Lord Jesus Christ. Praise His holy Name.

Whether you feel weak or discouraged, you are victorious. You must maintain your mind and heart attitude, by thinking victory always. You must always speak victory and not defeat. Always tell yourself that everything is fine with you. You are healed, you are well. Your business is successful. You will live and not die. Everything will be with you according to the Word of God.

You must not magnify your limitations and human capabilities, which are prone to failure. If you continue to look at yourself from this humanly perspective, you will continue undermining yourself and only ascribing victory to the Lord Jesus. The Apostle Paul said to the Corinthians that we do not look at people according to who they are in the flesh because when anyone is in Christ, he is a new creature (2 Corinthians 5:16-17). Please do not misunderstand me here: the Lord Jesus is victorious, indeed, and yes, victory belongs to Him, but He gives us this victory. He does not lend it to us for a short period, He gives it to us permanently. Victory in every area of your life, is yours, in the Lord Jesus.

There was a sure promise of victory for the people of God, in the Old Testament, under the law of Moses, for obedience to the law. The benefit of obedience, to the Old Testament laws and statutes, was elevation. God said to the children of Israel, *"If you obey, you will be the head and not the tail; above only and not beneath, and all the triumphant promises of God"* (Deuteronomy 28). Now you know that you and I are living under a better Covenant and better promises. The Israelite's Covenant was sealed by the blood of animals; our Covenant is sealed by the precious blood of the Holy Son of God, the Lord Jesus Christ.

In the New Testament, we obey the Lord Jesus' commandment of love, according to John 13:34.

> **A new commandment I give unto you, That ye love one another; as I have loved you, that ye also love one another.**

The commandment of love raises the bar higher than the commandments Moses gave to the children of Israel. If you love your neighbour, you will not lie, steal, kill, etc, against them. In fact, this new commandment of love will do in us what the Old Testament could not do – that is forgive. We are able to forgive just as God does because the love of God has been shed abroad in our hearts by the Holy Spirit

(Romans 5:5). God forgives by never remembering our sins. This is the ability that He has given to us as well. To forgive like He does. Not remembering the sins of others against us. If satan brings them to memory, we can boldly tell him, *"It never happened. All I have for that person is love."* The love that God has shed on our hearts does not keep a record of wrongs against anyone. So, if the things that people did to you keep coming to mind, be sure that they are not originating from you. You are like a magnet and people's wrongs are like paper. No matter how much you try to hold paper on a magnet, the magnet will not hold it. It is exactly the same with people's wrongs against you. The love in your heart cannot hold onto them. Someone has to hold them up in your face, to keep them before you, and that someone is satan. He loves it when you get angry about another person's wrong deeds against you because he knows that that is the only way to prevent your faith from taking you into victory. The Bible says that faith works by love – so, unforgiveness will prevent the victory securing faith to work for you and you will be defeated. Do not let satan do that to you.

You must walk in love and fulfil the royal law of love, according to the Scriptures (James 2:8). When you walk in love, you will experience the blessings of obedience, according to the Old Testament and more.

With the love of God in you, you are the head and not the tail. You are above only and not beneath. Your enemies will come after you in one direction, but they will scatter in seven. Praise the Name of the Lord. You will experience victory upon victory, and nothing shall be impossible with you.

I have always had an attitude of victorious thinking, which I got from my late Dad. I gave my life to the Lord Jesus when I was fifteen years old. I was in grade eight, at that time. In the first year, when I gave my life to the Lord, I read the Bible through once, from cover to cover, and I continued reading it through once every year. I grew so fast in the Lord that I became Chairman of our high school Scripture Union towards the end of grade ten. This was the first time, during my high school years, that a grade ten student was elected to become Chairman of the Scripture Union. The tradition was that elections for the committee members would be held in the last school term. The incumbent Chairman would be a grade twelve, who would only have a few months to stay on, and then they would choose a grade eleven, who was already in the committee as Chairman. However, when the time came for selecting the new committee, in the year when I was in grade ten, I was selected as Chairman.

CHAPTER 4

I have always grown-up taking God at His Word. There are many times where I had failed to receive what I was aiming for and, in all these circumstances, God would show me my mistakes and I would quickly repent and get back on the victory side. As a young believer, I always insisted on getting good grades. I was always in the top ten, right through school. I loved to take challenging subjects in school and asked God for wisdom to get good grades. When I was in Grade 8, I remember the senior students would always scare and discourage us concerning Technical Drawing. My attitude has always been, *"There is nothing impossible with my God and there is nothing impossible with me when I believe in God."* So, I went into my Technical Drawing class with the attitude that, *"I will show you who is boss."* And for sure, I got a distinction in Technical Drawing at Grade 9. My first year in the School of Natural Sciences, at University, was also the same. We were told by those, who had gone before us, that we would fail Physics. Yet again, I particularly brought Physics before God and said, *"Lord, show Yourself strong on my behalf."* For my final result, I got a distinction in Physics.

God has said that you are the head; you must insist on being the head and not the tail. You have the Holy Spirit, the Helper. The Lord Jesus said, *"When the Holy Spirit comes, He will bring to remembrance the things I have taught you"* (John 14:26). He does not only remind you of the teachings of the Lord Jesus, He also reminds you of everything you have learnt and studied. Ask Him to do this for you. He will help you in everything. He will give you wisdom in all manners of learning, like He gave to the four Hebrew children (Daniel 1:17).

One important thing you need to remember, is that the Holy Spirit is the Helper. He will help you in doing what you need to do. When you are studying, you need to commit what you are studying to your memory. When your memory fails, the Helper will be there to help you. Do not expect Him to read for you or do all the work for you, while you are lazing around. He is the Helper, and a helper is not the main doer of the work; the helper supports the main doer.

In a class of many believers and other hard-working sinners, there could be people who will perform better than you. That is okay. The head ends at the chin, so I am happy with a fifth position in a class of about forty students; I am still the head. However, I will not settle for failure. This is not to say that I have not failed before. Yes, I have, but in all those instances, I was disobedient and took my eyes off the Lord and, like Peter, I began to sink. When I realised my sin and repented, the Lord raised me up again and granted me victory. We will talk about falling short of the glory of God in another chapter later.

The Lord is gracious in every circumstance. He will not let you down. When you cry out for help and repent of your sin, He will reach out and save you and place you in your victory lane again. When you attempt to do what you had failed at before, you will be guaranteed victory when you put the Lord before you.

You must always see yourself the way God sees you. God sees you as His own child, with the characteristics of Himself, which are victorious and unconquerable. We have taken on the identity of the Lord Jesus Christ and, therefore, we can never be defeated.

> ***Herein is our love made perfect, that we may have boldness in the day of judgment: because as he is, so are we in this world.***
> ***1 John 4:17***

The last part of this verse says, "*... as He (Jesus) is, so are we in this world.*" It is how He *is* and not how He *was*. When He walked on the face of this Earth, Jesus was a man born under the law and subject to the ordinances and regulations of this world. To understand the two aspects of the Lord Jesus, let us look at the type of these prototypes in the Old Testament. The Israelites had been complaining against Moses because they needed water at Rephidim, so God tells Moses to go and strike a rock and the Rock was to bring out water (Exodus 17). Moses obeys God; he goes and strikes the Rock, and it yields water. This is the same Rock that followed them in the wilderness and the next time that the Israelites complained and wanted water at Zin (Numbers 20), God told Moses to speak to the Rock, so that it could give out water for the people. Moses, for reasons known to himself, decided to disobey the instructions; instead of speaking to the Rock, he struck it again, like he did at Rephidim! God was angry with Moses and judged him, saying that he would not enter the Promised Land. The Rock, who is the Lord Jesus, was only to be stricken once for our sins (Hebrews 6:4-6).

While on Earth, in His physical body, the Lord Jesus could be stricken and afflicted when He became sin for us. However, in His glorified state, no one can dare lay a finger on Him. This is the state we are in – as He is. That is why the Lord Jesus said to us, *"Nothing shall by any means hurt you"* (Luke 10:19). He further says in John 16:33 (AMPC), *"… in this world you will have tribulations… but take courage… I have deprived it of the power to harm you and have conquered it for you."* Praise the Name of the Lord. We are on the victory side. The world cannot conquer us. Satan and all his demons cannot conquer us. People who rise up against us, will fall for our sake. If your enemies have half a brain, they should make peace with you and not put you on a *wanted* list. Your defender is the Creator of the Heavens and the Earth, and He will defend you, and once He is done, a notice will be sent out to all those who were planning to rise up against you.

We can never undermine the importance of realising that the victory, that we are talking about, is only in the Lord Jesus. When a child of God understands their Kingdom rights and starts to pursue what belongs to them, satan will then offer them other ways in achieving success and victory. You must be careful not to take these.

When the Lord Jesus was about to start His ministry on Earth, satan offered Him the kingdoms of this world and their glory, if Jesus would worship him (Matthew 4). Of course, the Lord Jesus refused satan's offer and went ahead in achieving authority over the kingdoms of this world God's way. We have read this story up until the end and we know that, in the end, the Lord Jesus took over all authority in Heaven and on Earth; and He took the keys of hades, which gives Him authority under the Earth, thus giving Jesus complete dominion in the three realms. However,

Jesus was only able to achieve this by using God's methods for succeeding: living as a man, going to the cross, dying, rising again on the third day and, thereby, obtaining a greater Name. Had the Lord chosen to worship satan, in order to get the glories of the kingdoms of this world, His victory could not have been achieved.

This offer, from satan, is always presented anyone, in God, who set out to do great things for God. Satan comes through and gives them an alternative, to the methods of God, for achieving greatness in ministry, in business or in general life. Alas, a number of God's people fall for this scheme. They choose satan's offer, sell their souls to him and receive short term success but their success does not last long. Satan's offer has an expiry date on it. Once that expiry date is over, he will take his property away.

As you set out to do great things for God, please be careful to not take the easy and corrupt way in order to succeed. If you have already done things that are ungodly, in your dealings, turn away in repentance, so that the Lord can help you and deliver you from the hold of satan. Let God lead you and He will make your victory sweet.

The church of the Lord Jesus Christ is not in a defensive mode, hiding from the enemy. We are in an offensive mode, clad with the full armour of God. We do not sit in our homes, protecting our lives from enemy invasion with electric fencing all around. We are out in the streets, in the ghettos, and in every place where man is found. We do so with full assurance that we are safe and secure. We look for every place where the devil has held rebellion to the lordship of the Lord Jesus Christ. We undo his works and chase him out, announcing to his prisoners that the Lord Jesus has come to set them free.

We are not here for self-preservation because we are certain of our livelihood. Ours is to pursue a rescue mission of those that satan has kept in the shadow of death. We are not fighting to stay alive because the Lord is our life and the length of our days. We are overflowing with life and vitality and the life in us, flows to those around us, to give them this life.

Nothing shall deter us from enforcing our God-given victory over every aspect of God's creation. We will not retreat from the command the Lord Jesus – the Commander in Chief – gave to us. He said, *"Go,"* and we will go in His name. His command is valid in times of war and in times of peace. It is valid in times of a pandemic and in times of health.

CHAPTER 5

YOU MUST BE BORN AGAIN

Human beings are capable of accomplishing great things here on Earth, even without coming to the saving knowledge of the Lord Jesus. However, these accomplishments will not benefit them in eternity. The Lord Jesus said that a man will not have any profit, if he were to own the whole world and lose his soul (Mark 8:36). People are capable of having great accomplishments on their own. The blessing that God pronounced on human beings, at the beginning of man's creation, still stands on every person today – saved or unsaved.

The only tragedy, for an unsaved successful person, is that their success is limited to this natural world. Our lives, in this world, are finite. They have a beginning and an end. Real success, therefore, must outlive our finite lives here on Earth. There is a hell to avoid and a Heaven to gain. We must remember that no matter how distant we are from thinking about God, we will one day stand before Him and give an account for the deeds done here on Earth. If you, therefore, live a successful life here on Earth and end up in an eternity without God, you are a loser. Therefore, I am not going to concentrate on the success that people see outside of the Lord Jesus. On the other hand, it is also important to note that children of God can also have tremendous natural success. The best, therefore, is to have natural and spiritual success.

I know that there are many theories that people have developed, and they have cushioned themselves in these theories that either deny the existence of God or the existence of eternal punishment of sinners. They engage in debates, to discredit the integrity of the Word of God, so they can sooth their guilty consciences. This debate is directly linked to the integrity of the Lord Jesus because the Lord Jesus taught about hell and Heaven. If the Lord Jesus is the divine Son of God, we must accept His teachings as truth and be guided by them. He made very bold and powerful statements, which could only be made by God or by some highly confused dreamer. The Lord Jesus has proven Himself, as the divine Son of God, by His resurrection from the dead. His life and the miracles He did while He lived on Earth, all testify of His Deity. Therefore, friends, we must believe Him and rely on every word He has spoken. The Lord Jesus is not a confused dreamer, like some cult leaders who have ended up sending their followers to an early death. The Lord Jesus is God manifested in the flesh. We must listen to what He has to say.

The starting point is receiving the Lord Jesus Christ as the Lord and Saviour of your life. When you give your life to the Lord Jesus, and become born again, you step into a Godkind of life that brings with it victories that you could not experience outside of the Lord Jesus.

Being born again is an experience that is referred to using various terminologies in the Word of God, but it means the same thing. Once you have received the Lord Jesus Christ as your Lord and Saviour, you are made into a new creature from that moment on. You confess Jesus as the Lord of your life and He indeed becomes Lord. It is as simple as that. The confession from your mouth, that Jesus is Lord, creates the reality that He is Lord in your life. Therefore, Christianity is called the great confession (Hebrews 3:1, Hebrews 4:14).

All the statements, of the restoration of our relationship with God, will point to the establishment of the Lordship of Jesus Christ over our lives.

It may be called repenting, according to Acts 2:38. Repentance means to change one's mind or purpose. It is the type of change of mind that the prodigal son had, in the parable that the Lord Jesus spoke about, in Luke 15. The son changed his mind about the place he had gone to, he decided to do something about it and returned to his father. It is turning from sin to the Lord – that is what repentance means. The Bible says, *"Turn to the Lord"* (Hosea 14:2). There is no repentance without corresponding positive action, in order to align to a new way of thinking. If there is no action, there is no repentance; you are merely thinking about it.

In Acts 2:38, Peter told his hearers that they must repent and be baptised. Baptism is the outward declaration of what has happened to someone inwardly. So, for these people to act on their repentance, they were told to demonstrate it by being baptised in the Name of the Lord Jesus. I know that there are some people who teach that there is no salvation without baptism, while others start baptising everyone they see in order to try and get them saved. Baptism, in itself, does not save anyone. Someone must make a decision to receive the Lord Jesus as Saviour, and only then will baptism mean something to them.

CHAPTER 5

The other statement, used for restoring a person's relationship to the Heavenly Father, is being born again. Jesus, in John 3:7, said to Nicodemus, *"... you must be born again."* The apostle Peter also says to his hearers.

> **Being born again, not of corruptible seed, but of incorruptible, by the word of God, which liveth and abideth for ever.**
> **1 Peter 1:23 KJV**

This is the most used statement, to express the transformation that takes place, when we are changed from being a child of satan to a child of God. We are born again. We become a completely brand new person. You see, the new birth, which we experience upon receiving the Lord Jesus as Saviour, is a new experience that creates in us a brand new person. Bear in mind that you and I are spirit beings. Therefore, when we become new, God puts in us a new spirit. What happens to the old spirit? That old spirit died with the Lord Jesus Christ. When we get dipped in the waters of baptism, we demonstrate his burial. When we are raised in the water, we demonstrate our resurrection to a new life. God promised to put a new spirit in us. He does this at the point we become born again.

You must realize that when you are born again, your past is no longer counted against you. You are a different person. The person who committed the sins, is dead. The person who is now alive in you, is a new person (2 Corinthians 5:21). If the devil reminds you of the past sins, tell him that you never committed them. If you sin as a child of God, it is not your born again human spirit that is behind these sins. In fact, the new you can never sin. Because you are born of God (1 John 3:9). When sin happens in the life of a believer, we yield our members to it, to do its desires. It is like you lending your vehicle to someone else to drive it recklessly. That person is not the rightful owner, but you have given them permission to use your vehicle. For as long as you allow them to use it, they will do whatever they want with the vehicle, until you tell them to stop and return it.

You are not the reckless driver, they are. You are still the law-abiding citizen that you are. You could, however, suffer some consequences, if the abuse of your car was done with your permission. In the same way, you are not the sinner, your old self is. You are still the righteousness of God (2 Peter 5:21)

Sin is no longer our master. We died to sin. When we sin, therefore, we give in to sin's demands and let it use our bodies. Sin does not come from our spiritual nature anymore, as it did before we became born again. That is why the best way to overcome any sinful habit, is to continually treat yourself as the righteousness of God. It does not matter what you have done. Do not allow the label of a sinner, to be yours. You are a saint. There are times we identify ourselves, from a natural standpoint, with the rest of mankind as sinners. This is only relevant when you are relating to people who have not yet received the Lord Jesus as Saviour. I have said this as well. Like Paul, I become all things to all me, so that I may save some (2 Corinthians 9:22).

Salvation, by receiving the Lord Jesus as Saviour and Lord, is the greatest possession that one can have in this life. You could reach the highest level of education, own the biggest number of assets, attaint the highest sports and entertainment awards, become the world's number one billionaire, but if you do not have the Lord Jesus as your Saviour, then you are the biggest loser that has ever lived.

The Apostle John asks this question:

> ***Who is he that overcometh the world, but he that believeth that Jesus is the Son of God?***
> ***1 John 5:5 KJV***

We have victory over the world. This victory comes by believing in the Lord Jesus. When you become born again, you are raised to a level of authority, where the Lord Jesus is seated in the Heavenly places. You become a child of God and God becomes your Father. You become one with God because God puts His life in you.

You must insist on experiencing the life of God, not only in your spirit, but also in your soul and body. God comes to live in your spirit. Your spirit is in your physical body and, therefore, God lives in your body. It is His house. Let the life of God radiate from your spirit into your soul and body. Do not allow sickness to settle in and be comfortable in your body. Release the power of God from inside of you to bring life to every part of your being. The release of God happens through our mouth. Confess who you are and what rightfully belongs to you, as a child of God. Tell your body that it is healed now – not in the future. Faith is in the *now*. Tell yourself that you are prosperous now – not after you finish your degree and get a job. Know your rights and privileges in the Lord Jesus and confess these over your life, your family, your ministry, and everything that concerns you. Keep the Word of God before your eyes and listen to faith words. These will reach your mind and help it start thinking in line with who you are in the Lord.

CHAPTER 5

These are the benefits of the new birth. The Godhead lives on the inside of you. They are not there to count how many times you fall. They are there to be God through you. They want to express themselves in a life that is yielding to them. Friends, when you learn to hear the voice of the Holy Spirit and obey His leading, you will be unstoppable.

CHAPTER 6
STEP UP TO GOD'S GLORY

When God made man, He made him to experience His glory. Glory is a multifaceted word, which has various meanings in the Bible. It refers to honour, splendour, majesty, beauty, weight, comeliness, excellency, dignity, and many others. All these explanations, of glory, refer to areas of a victorious life. When people become victorious in their lives, in their line of work or in their careers, they then describe their accomplishments using one or more of these words. When one attains great grades in their academic qualifications, they are said to have received academic excellence. Anyone, who rules over others, is referred to as *your majesty*. Parliamentarians are referred to as honourable members. All these are expressions of glory, which expresses dominance and complete authority over the relevant circumstances.

We have been given a position of dominance and excellence, by virtue of our standing in the Lord Jesus. The Holy Spirit wrote the following through the Apostle Paul:

> *But God, who is rich in mercy, for his great love wherewith he loved us, Even when we were dead in sins, hath quickened us together with Christ, (by grace ye are saved;) And hath raised us up together, and made us sit together in heavenly places in Christ Jesus...*
> *Ephesians 2:4-6 KJV*

We have been made to sit with the Lord Jesus in the Heavenly places. This place, where we are seated with the Lord Jesus, is explained further in verse 1 of the same Epistle.

> *Which he wrought in Christ, when he raised him from the dead, and set him at his own right hand in the heavenly places, Far above all principality, and power, and might, and dominion, and every name that is named, not only in this world, but also in that which is to come: And hath put all things under his feet, and gave him to be the head over all things to the church, Which is his body, the fulness of him*

that filleth all in all.
Ephesians 1:20-23 KJV

This place is on the right hand of the Father. It is a place of authority and absolute power. We are sitting in a place of superiority to all forces of darkness and every authority of satan. To add to this, the Lord Jesus has been given headship, over all things, to the church. Other versions of the Bible say, *"... for the church..."* The Lord Jesus has authority over everything, for the benefit of the church. He is head of media, sport, education, economy, entertainment, politics, etc. There is nothing, therefore, in the universe that can resist the advance of the church of the Lord Jesus Christ. This is because the head, of them all, is the Lord, Who is head of the church. He will see to it that every sector of human existence opens to the advances of His church. It is this church that He spoke about in the Gospel of Matthew 16:18 – *"I will build my church and the gates of hell shall not prevail against it."*

The secret is that you must make your advance for dominance, in the sector of life, where you have been called. Satan may be in possession of those sectors but he is not the rightful owner and, therefore, your advance to take over those areas will succeed. Satan will not stop you. He will resist and try to hold on to what is not his through rebellion, but your persistent faith will take it away from him and bring it into your possession.

You have victory over every circumstance that is contrary to your success. Understand this and continually declare it out loud:

- I have victory over the economic sector of this world.

- I am successful in my business dealings and every deal that I make, will work out in my favour.

- The Holy Spirit directs my every footstep and leads me to places of victory and success in every area of my life.

- I have favour with God and man.

Your standard of measure is what is in Heaven and not what is here on Earth. The Earth will go through cycles of challenges and if you base your success on the Earth's cycles, your dominance will be dependent on the decisions of politicians and economists. But lift your eyes and see the bounty of your Heavenly Father. He has more than enough ways and means to cause you to succeed. You will flourish in an economy that is poorly managed by politicians. Just acknowledge the Lord Jesus as Head over all things. Do

CHAPTER 6

not blame the politicians, rather put a demand on your Heavenly Father to show Himself strong on your behalf.

This does not mean that you should shun politics and only pray. No. Doing this would be like trying to drive a car on one wheel. You need to focus on every area of life and let the Lord Jesus take His rightful place in each one of those areas. If a country is being mismanaged by politicians, then look out for the believers who have been called into the political sector and support them, so that their voices can be heard. Do the same with the media and all the other sectors of life. Pray and do something about it. If you are called into one of these areas, go in and make a difference; if not, support the children of God who are called into these sectors. If there are no children of God there, go in and preach Christ to those who are in there. When they receive the Lord Jesus as Saviour, they will turn to Him and represent Him in their respective sector.

Sometimes, evil overtakes a nation and circumstances and become unbearable for both the child of God and unconverted; it overtakes everyone. Be sensitive to the direction of God. He may tell you to save up for the years of famine, or He may tell you to move from one country to another. Whatever the situation, God takes care of His own.

The triumph of the church, over every sector of life, is applicable to both the church at large and individual believers. You have the authority, through God, to excel to the highest level of achievement, in every human endeavour that you are involved in. This is because of the Lord Jesus, Who gives you the strength to accomplish great things for His glory. If your passion is in ministry, step out and obey the calling of God on your life. The Lord Jesus is the head over the Christian ministry, and He will see to it that you succeed in what you do. If it is business, step out and trust God for great opportunities to come your way. If your passion is in media, sport, entertainment, or whichever area, go into it knowing that you have been empowered by God to succeed. Make confessions of success because you are working with the Lord, Who made the Heavens and Earth, and He never fails.

Children of God only experience defeat when they take their focus from the great possibilities that God can do through them and they focus on the limitations of human strength that they have. Remember that you are not an ordinary person. You have God living inside you. He is not there to be a passenger, or baggage or a silent listener to every conversation – no. He is there to do life with you. Allow God to express Himself through you. Let Him be

God in you, so that through Him, you can do those things that only God can do.

Our legal position, before God, is the position where we are seated with the Lord Jesus in the Heavenly places. We are first and foremost residents of Heaven. That is why the Bible says, *"Of course, we are living in the world, but we do not wage war in a world-like way"* (2 Corinthians 10:3 ISV). Why? Because our citizenship is in Heaven (Philippians 3:20 ISV). We must look at what is available in Heaven and pray that it will be the same for us here on Earth. There is no poverty in Heaven, so poverty is not your portion. There is no premature death in heaven, so you will not die early. There is no slavery in Heaven, so you are a free. There are no business failures in Heaven, so your business will thrive. There is no sickness in Heaven, so you are healed.

I know that there could be some who may have heard the song that God will not share glory with any man, so, let us deal with that topic so that we can be on the same page. When we understand the meaning of glory, we then realise that it is one of the things that people seek after in life. I have seen people who have given up highly paid jobs, in order to take up positions in politics that does not pay as much but has great honour attached to them. They suspend their money-making ventures to get the glory of men.

Glory opens doors for you that will bring in more money than what you would get from mere hard work. A person attributed with excellence (glory) will be sought out by kings. So, people of this world seek after glory. Would God then withhold this from His children? No. I will show you from the Word of God that God loves to give His people glory.

When Solomon asked the Lord for wisdom, to rule the people of Israel, God not only gave him the wisdom he had asked for, He also gave him riches, wealth and honour along with it (2 Chronicles 1:12). God is not intimidated by men sharing in His glory. In fact, the opposite is true; He gives it out to His children. The Psalmist said:

> **For the LORD God is a sun and shield: the LORD will give grace and glory: no good thing will he withhold from them that walk uprightly.**
> **Psalm 84:11**

You are designed to experience God's glory in every area of your life. Yours is to experience honour and not shame or disrespect, splendour and not insignificance, and so on. You are meant to achieve the best and most excellent results of your doings, so that you can experience excellence. You are going to be recognised everywhere you go and given medals of excellence because God's glory is upon you. All these measures of glory belong to God and they come from Him alone. Satan will not place you on a pedestal, in order to celebrate you. It is God Who crowns you with glory. The Psalmist further says:

> ***For thou hast made him a little lower than the angels, and hast crowned him with glory and honour.***
> ***Psalm 8:5***

This glory, that we have been crowned with, is the glory of God. You already have glory on you. You have honour, beauty, excellence, dignity, and everything that comes with exceptional performance, even before you make your first step in trying to achieve something in life. The Lord Jesus reinforced your position of glory when He prayed to the Father and made an affirmative statement to this effect:

> ***And the glory which thou gavest me I have given them; that they may be one, even as we are one…***
> ***John 17:22***

Jesus has given us the Father's glory. We have God the Father's excellence, honour, and abilities, so that we may be one, in Him. These are powerful people of God. When you realise that you and your brother, or sister next door, have the glory of God, you will not need to compete with them. You will seek to compliment them, so that your God-given excellence, and theirs, can combine, in order to do something greater for God. You will refuse every form of slavery and domination, from other people, because you also have the right to walk in the Father's glory, just like any other person who has accepted the Lord Jesus as Saviour. They might be your boss, but you are one with them before God. You can take instructions from them, but they cannot demean your God-given dignity as His child.

You must expect to walk in God's glory everywhere you go and in whatever you do. The glory of God will make you pass through hostile crowds that have risen up against you. Jesus did this when men took Him to a mountain cliff, so that they could throw Him down headlong. The Bible says the glory of the Lord shall be our rear guard (Isaiah 58:8). A rear guard is a unit of soldiers that go behind the attacking units, in order to provide cover for them from the rear. The glory will provide a covering for your rear in all matters of life. If someone tries to stab you from the back – and you will find many backstabbers in life – the glory will protect you. Glory to God.

What I am talking about, is experienced when someone realises what belongs to them and takes it for themselves. The Lord Jesus told Martha, the sister of Lazarus who had died:

> ***Jesus saith unto her, Said I not unto thee, that, if thou wouldest believe, thou shouldest see the glory of God?***
> ***John 11:40***

You must believe. You need not only realise that the glory of God is yours to help you succeed in all situations that may be humanly impossible, you must also think and confess as such. In the glory of God, there is honour and not shame, there is victory and not defeat, there is power and not weakness, and there is manifestation of His presence all the time.

The cloud of God's presence, which filled the temple of Solomon, is always with us, and in us, and we will take It wherever we go. With the glory of God upon us, we do not have to wait for God to move. Wherever we move to, God comes right along with us because that is His promise. He said, *"I will be with you wherever you go until the close of the age."* The age has not closed yet, so we must continue moving and taking the glory of God wherever we go. When

God's glory is in any place, God will do great things among the people to confirm our message.

Our lives move from glory to glory (2 Corinthians 3:18). There is no time for being docile and unproductive. You can never be pushed into a place of ineffectiveness when you are in the Lord Jesus. Do we sometimes get discouraged? Yes, we do. But we must never forget who we are and what we have. We are carriers of God. He lives in us and He is able to do much more in us.

We have seen that God has given us His glory. However, unbelief will certainly cause us to fail in attaining the glory of God. The Bible says that sin makes us fall short of the glory of God (Romans 3:23). Unbelief is one such sin. The problem with unbelief, is that it can be contagious. Unbelief expresses itself in thoughts, actions, and words. When it is expressed in actions and words, it will affect those who see the action and hear those words of unbelief. When people go into unbelief, and they are too proud to admit that they are, they start creating a standard of life that is below the glory of God. If these people are church leaders, then they start to teach this unbelief to their congregations and before you realise it, the whole congregation is walking in unbelief and living below the standards of God's glory. We have used Romans 3:23 to lead sinners to the Lord Jesus Christ, but we must also use it for the saints who are walking in unbelief. Unbelief will cause you to fall short of the glory of God.

As preachers, we need to understand that we do not know everything. We need to be open to learn from others and let other people, who understand a particular concept better, teach us. We may have huge titles and wear robes, but we may not operate in a particular teaching anointing, which we will need, when our time of need comes. While I am talking about this, I should also mention that preachers need to work with other preachers who have a similar, or even higher, ministry anointing as them. There are times when you need a prayer of agreement for certain things that you need. If you are the only one who pours yourself out for others, and standing in prayer for others, and you do not have anyone else to preach faith to you when you need to hear it, you may fall short. When I purposed to live the life of faith, I began to notice, among my fellow believers, that there are not many people who I can call upon to pray the prayer of agreement with me. This is sad. Many believers pray, what they call *the prayer of faith*, but then they go talking about the person they prayed for, *"That person is in big trouble. We have prayed and we are trusting God for them."* I do not want these types of people to know anything about what I am going through; they are not believing God. The are doubting God and their prayer is a waste of time.

CHAPTER 7
FIND THE THIEF

When you know what rightfully belongs to you, and you experiencing loss of that, you must find out who is responsible for stealing your belongings. We have seen the good things that have been given to us through the death, burial, resurrection, and assentation of our Lord Jesus. When any of these things are taken away from us, we must know who took them.

Restoration comes when the thief is caught. The Bible says:

> *Men do not despise a thief, if he steal to satisfy his soul when he is hungry; But if he be found, he shall restore sevenfold; he shall give all the substance of his house.*
> *Proverbs 6:30-31*

Note that the thief only pays back if he is found. If he has not been found, there will be no restoration. This is a very important point to remember. There are many people who are entertaining thieves in their homes and these thieves continue plundering resources from them. Some of these thieves are probably people you have come to know and like. They take advantage of your kindness and start sucking life resources out of you. Instead of confronting them as thieves, many of us even start making excuses for them and blame everyone else except for these individuals. It happens a lot in romantic relationships, where one of the parties starts exploiting the other, and takes advantage, because of the relationship that exists between the two. I have seen young women get into a place of despair because they continued to entertain a man whose intention was to suck life resources out of them. It is not because these women do not know about what their partner is doing or can do but, rather, it is because they overlook the person's actions, and blame everybody else apart from the culprit. A thief must be caught and identified as such if restoration must happen.

The same thing is required in marriage if you desire a victorious marriage. You must identify the little foxes, as stated in the Song of Solomon 2:15. If your partner's coming home late every night is causing you to be offended, you must raise this topic and address it. *Catching the little foxes* means raising the areas of conflict or discomfort that happens in your marriage relationship and discussing them, as husband and wife. You cannot wish them away or wait for them to disappear. They must be arrested through a structured conversation, addressed, and dealt with. If your partner is doing something that is hurting you, or is unpleasant to you, you must find time to talk about it. Confronting these issues will most likely result in a conflict. This is because even the best of us has those irritating characteristics that we call blind spots. They are blind spots because we are not aware of how irritating they can become to someone. The fact that we are not aware that other people, especially the people we love, get irritated by the things we do, will most definitely cause a negative reaction from us when confronted.

Every one of us has a great self-image. However, when we are confronted with facts about how other people view us and the image our actions create for us, we will be shocked and become either angry or disappointed. That is why marriage related issues, that bring discomfort to either party, must be discussed in a safe environment of love and understanding. The fact, however, is that these issues must be addressed and dealt with decisively. If marriage issues are left unaddressed, they will breed conflict and may lead to a defeated marriage.

It is vital to identify the issue correctly here. The issue is the *action* and not the *actor*. So, regarding the topic of this chapter, the thief that must be arrested is the *action* of your partner and not your partner, themselves. When your partner does something that brushes you the wrong way, you have every right to express your feelings in this same manner – address the *action* and not the *actor*. How do you do that? Let us say, for example, your partner said something to you, in the presence of your friends, that made you feel undermined. When addressing this, you would say, *"I felt undermined by that statement you made..."* You are addressing the statement and what you felt. This statement allows dialogue to start without pre-judging the intentions of your partner. It will give them a chance to explain themselves and make amends in a love environment. If you say, *"You undermined me when you made that statement..."* You have already judged that your partner had wrong intentions and, as a natural stance, your partner will start to defend themselves.

The *action* of your spouse is what you must address, and put measures in place, to help each other to do things differently. The partner who caused offense may or may not have had the intention to offend. Whatever the case, reacting with an attack on the person is aiming for the wrong enemy and be sure that peace will not come by that. Always aim for the correct target. This does not mean that people should not take accountability for their action. There are many times when people become spiteful and aim to hurt their partners. If the issue was brought about intentionally, the confrontational approach is still the same. The one who caused wrong will need to confess the wrong they have done and ask for forgiveness.

We must understand that when couples start to address each other and demean each other, when trying to resolve an issue in their marriage, they let the actual *thief* go free and they catch the wrong guy. With that, a victorious marriage relationship will be difficult to attain.

CHAPTER 8
LOVE YOUR WAY TO VICTORY

Love is the most powerful force to overcome every human relation challenge. Aggression and anger have only led people into enmity, which have destroyed lives and left children destitute. If we can learn that the use of love, and all the characteristics it represents, causes broken relationships to be mended, estranged loved ones to be restored, arch enemies to be reconciled, then we would opt to use love instead of hate, in every circumstance. Even the worst enemy, when treated with love, will have their defences crumble. Love is a product of the born again human spirit, which makes the person exhibiting it, to have beauty inside and outside.

The cruellest people are victims of a loveless background and so, the best way to deal with them, is to show them love. When you respond with aggression towards a cruel person, you feed the monster of hatred that has been developed in them, by the experience they went through. If, on the other hand, you respond with love, you start removing their cruelty. The Bible calls it *"...overcoming evil with good"* (Romans 12:21).

Love is not a feeling; it is a state of being. Look at the famous *love chapter* from 1 Corinthians 13 and you will see the things that love is or, rather, the things that people who love are – they are kind, peaceful, etc. All these are a state of being. You do not feel kind. It is either you are kind, or you are not. These are a state of being and we are born with all these traits.

Loves seeks good for the object of its love. Many people, today, take feelings of emotions as love. When they feel sexually attracted to a person, they call it love. That is not love. Sexual desire looks at satisfying the sexual appetites of one's self. Love does not look at satisfaction of self, but rather satisfaction of the other person. In relationships, it is always a good idea to ask, *"What would the person I love want out of my relationship with them?"* When you find the answer to this question, then pursue the things that your loved one wants and not your own wants. The best arrangement, in a relationship, is when each party is pursuing the other's joy and not their own. This is what is called being selfless in your relationship. Strife enters a relationship when the parties in the relationship become self-centred.

Love will love enough to let go. One of the decisions that made King Solomon stand out, as the wisest king that had ever lived, is the decision he made after giving *the love test* to the women who were fighting over a child (1 Kings 3). Because they could not decide who was the real mother of the child, the one woman agreed to have the child cut in half, so that they could share the child. The real mother, however, loved the child so much that she was prepared to let the child go to the other woman, if the child was left alive. People who say to you, *"If I cannot have you then nobody will,"* do not love you at all. Such people are haters and abusers. If you have a way of finding out that this is how they feel about you, find a way to stay away from them. True love will let a persistent loved one have their way, but love will not give up on hoping for their safe return to be reunited with them.

Love continues, even when it has been betrayed. The Lord Jesus persisted with love, even through the gruesome death He went through, and demonstrated His love for all men, including those who nailed Him to the cross. The Bible says this of the Roman Officer, who saw such great love in the face of the Master: when the Roman Military Officer, who was standing right in front of Jesus, saw how He died, he said, *"There is no doubt this man was the Son of God!"* (Mark 15:39 TPT). Love broke the barriers of cruelty, and a facade of *Mr Tough Guy*, and made the Centurion appreciate Who the Lord Jesus really is. This could happen between you and a cruel boss, or an estranged spouse. When you persist, in love, towards them, no matter what they have done, they will have no choice but to proclaim that, *"Surely this person is a real asset to the company,"* or, *"Surely this person really loves me."*

I have said, previously, that we must ensure that when we pray for our enemies, we align our prayers to the New Testament pattern. The Old Testament pattern was usually seeking vengeance against enemies. The New Testament is different. We see the good of all people – friend or foe. Why? Because we are on the victory side of love and on this side, love conquers all things. We have seen *the love Scripture*, in 1 Corinthians 13, and we see that there is nothing impossible in the achievement of successful human relationships if we do it the love way.

Sometimes we imagine love to be some complicated attitude of the mind and tolerance of bad behaviour. It is rather good old kindness, giving a helping hand; being generous with what you have; holding back on words that could hurt the other person; retraining yourself from causing pain on someone when you feel you should do so; forgiving those who have wronged you, and so on. Friend, love is the most natural way to react to another person. Every other way is learnt, rehearsed, and planned, but love does not need to be planned. If you are yourself, love will naturally spring out of your heart to reach the other person. You will hardly find a school of love around the world. Evil people go out of their way to teach others how to hate. Governments around the world, who practiced different types of prejudice against certain races, had to indoctrinate their followers first, before their followers turned on their fellow humans. All these forms of hatred had to be overcome by love. The initiation of evil is always people who listen to the lies of satan – just like what Eve did in the garden of Eden.

Right throughout history, love has always conquered hatred. When a whole generation of people have been indoctrinated to hate, there will come a generation that will grow up in an environment where there is no such indoctrination and, sooner or later, the hate will be dethroned.

When you are born again, you have the love of God poured out in your heart by the Holy Spirit (Roman 5:5). This love helps you to love the way God loves – unconditionally, despite the other person's flaws. The love of God, for other believers, does not wait for people to agree on all the doctrinal issues. We love one another and demonstrate this love, by doing good by our brothers and sisters in the Lord, working with them in the ministry and looking out for their good. We do this even when we know that they may be talking about us concerning our ministry.

CHAPTER 9

YOUR FAITH OVERCOMES THE WORLD

For whatsoever is born of God overcometh the world: and this is the victory that overcometh the world, even our faith.
1 John 5:4

Faith in God is so important that the whole Christian life is referred to as *the faith* (Acts 6:7). The early disciples, who believed in the Lord Jesus Christ, were said to be obedient to *the faith*. Faith in God is, simply, faith in His Word. A person of faith takes every word, that God has spoken, as truth. They act on it and live as if the Word of God is true and is a final authority. When you take God at His Word and live life with every action you take based on the knowledge that God's Word is true, you will be sure to achieve great results. You will always come out on top of every situation.

I have had to repent before the Lord for the way I had treated and taught about the written Word of God – the Bible. I used to say that the written Word is the letter that kills and that the words that will benefit you, are those that will *jump* off the pages of the Bible, as the Holy Spirit makes them alive. This, friends, is wrong and if you have heard me say this before, please forgive me. The Bible is God speaking to you and me. There are statements that have been written, as examples, so that we can see what other people went through, and there are those that have been written for our application. So, when you read the Bible and you see the words of God either directly, or through an inspired vessel, you must take it as the Lord is speaking to you. It is as if the Lord Jesus is sitting in your room with you and talking to you. That is why we must treat the written Word of God with great respect. Treat it with more respect than a poor man would treat the highest denomination of their currency, which had been given to them after days of starvation. They will hold dearly to that note and rush to the supermarket, or grocery store, to spend it. We must cherish the written Word of God and yearn to find a place where we can read, study, and hear the voice of our Master.

As we read and meditate on the Word, faith will come. Notice that *faith comes* by hearing. As long as you are hearing, or reading, the Word of God, faith will come, and you will grow in faith. The process of growth is slow and the person seeking growth, must be very patient. Just like we do not see our muscles growing, we will also not see our faith growing. However, just like exercise, for muscle growth, it requires consistency. We must be very consistent with studying the Word. When you are building your muscles in the gym, you do not move from lifting 10kg weights to 30kg weights. In fact, you must stay on the 10kg weight, until your muscles are strong enough to lift that small weight with ease. Then you move on to 11kg and increase progressively. If you take a break for a long time or you become inconsistent in going to the gym, you will stay on the 10kg weight or even drop to less than 10kg. This is the same with faith. Many of us are very inconsistent with listening to the Word of God and listening to faith messages. We start today and do it consistently for a week but then take a two-week break. This makes you lose even the little that you had built up in the first week. We must be consistent with the Word. When you are building your faith, read the portions of Scripture that will help you build your faith and then you can then read other stories. Make it a habit to read faith books and listen to faith tapes. If there is something you are believing God for, like healing, you should increase the intake of the Word and faith messages.

There are also some other important guidelines, in applying the Word of God, that are essential for the Word to become effective in our lives. To start with, we must understand the context that the Word was spoken in and ensure that we are applying it right. Many people take the Word of God out of its context and they end up making the Scriptures say whatever they want to hear. Be careful about that.

I remember when I was a young believer, I decided within myself that if Jesus could turn water into wine, I could also pray that water, filled into an empty pen tube, would be turned into ink. I, therefore, took an empty pen tube and filled it with water and went to the prayer room to pray that it be turned into ink. I prayed for an hour and then started to write the 23rd Psalm with the same pen. When I finished writing the Psalm, the pen stopped writing and never wrote again after that. When I got back to my class, where I needed to use the pen, someone gave me a new pen. There are some miracles in the Bible that were specific to people and if there is no clear directive, in the written Word of God, that such a miracle is a statement of fact or promise to you as a believer, you must receive a directive in form of a spoken instruction from the Holy Spirit to you, if you are expecting that miracle to happen in your life. There is no place in the Bible where it is written that believers shall turn water into wine, so you cannot set off, by faith, to turn water into anything, unless you have a direct revelation, or spoken word to your spirit, about the same. In the same way, there is no place in the Bible that says believers shall walk on water. The instruction to walk on water was given to one person – Peter. Notice that there were many disciples in the boat but none of them dared to step out, to go and have an on-the-water fellowship with the Lord Jesus. They all stayed put and only Peter, who was given the instruction, made the move to walk on the water. If the others had asked the Lord, He could have probably told them to also go to where He was, and they could have walked on the water on His Word.

When we do not have a specific word from the Lord Jesus, from the written Word, concerning something, we must spend time in prayer to ask Him if it is His will. When Heaven gives a *go ahead*, the peace of God is usually what covers your heart and mind. If there is no peace about that matter, then you better leave it alone.

Everything that is within the will of God, for His people, is revealed in the Word of God and is there for us to take it by faith. Healing has been given to us. We do not have to pray and ask if it is the will of God for us to be healed. We must just receive the healing by faith, in the written Word of God.

There is a lot of worldliness, today, that has crept into the lives of believers and that is why we do not get the results of obedience to the Word of God. Some of this worldliness is even being preached in the pulpits. I once heard a preacher encourage his hearers *to try God*. Now, when you come to God, to try Him out, after you have tried everything else, you will not get anything from God. The Bible says:

> **But without faith it is impossible to please him: for he that cometh to God must believe that he is, and that he is a rewarder of them that diligently seek him.**
> **Hebrews 11:6**

You do not come to God with the intention of trying Him out. Preachers must also not tell their congregations to try God. People who come to God, must believe that He is a rewarder of those who diligently seek Him. This means that when you come to God, you must know that you will get the help that you need. You come to Him with no other alternative. Coming to God, to try Him out, means that you have a *plan B,* just in case God does not meet your expectations. With this attitude, you must be sure that you will get nothing from Him, and you might as well begin with your *plan B*. The Bible further says:

CHAPTER 9

> ***O taste and see that the LORD is good: blessed is the man that trusteth in him.***
> ***Psalm 34:8 KJV***

Notice here that the Bible says, *"...taste and see **that** ..."* and not, *"...taste and see **if**..."* There is a big difference here. *"Taste and see **that**..."* means that when you step into His life, you will see that He is good, and you will have no choice to go anywhere else. If it had said, *"...taste and see **if**..."* we could then come to Him and if He is good enough for us, then we would stay on but if not, we would have the opportunity to go elsewhere. That is not the approach with which we approach God's Word.

When you need God to heal you, you do not go to God and ***try*** to get Him to heal you. With this attitude, you will be sentencing yourself to an early death. Go to God and know for sure that His Word works, and it will do in you what He said it will do. You are not coming to Him to ***try*** Him out, you are coming to Him, to receive what is yours. With this faith, you are guaranteed victory.

Let us deal with the statements, made by Queen Esther, in the book of Esther, as well as with the three Hebrew boys in the book of Daniel. When Queen Esther was convinced by

Mordecai to intercede for the Jews before King Ahasuerus, she made the following statement:

> *...and so will I go in unto the king, which is not according to the law: and if I perish, I perish.*
> *Esther 4:16b KJV*

Another statement of consecration was made by the Shadrach, Meshach, and Abednego when they were being forced to bow down to a golden image that had been made by the king of Babylon.

> *If it be so, our God whom we serve is able to deliver us from the burning fiery furnace, and he will deliver us out of thine hand, O king. But if not, be it known unto thee, O king, that we will not serve thy gods, nor worship the golden image which thou hast set up.*
> *Daniel 3:17-18 KJV*

Let us deal with Queen Esther's statement first. Queen Esther was going to undertake something that was contrary to the law of the land at the time. So, she was right to expect anything – even death. There was no given word or a guarantee that if she, as a queen, went into the king's chamber, at that time, that she could be pardoned. So, she committed to go and said to Mordecai, *"If I perish, I perish."* Our Heavenly Father is not like King Ahasuerus; He has given us His Word and invited us to come boldly to His Throne of Grace. When we come to His Throne of grace, **we will** find the help that we need. Queen Esther lived in the Old Covenant that was ratified by the blood of animals and God gave her favour in the sight of the king. Her petition was a matter of life and death. She entered the king's chamber and petitioned the king, and her petition was granted. We have a covenant ratified by the precious blood of the Lord Jesus. We have, therefore, been invited to come before our Heavenly Father boldly and state our problem. He will answer and deliver us with no option to perish.

The three Hebrew children were facing death, by a fiery furnace, without any spoken or written word of what God would do for them in the situation that they were in. So, they were justified in making the statement, *"God is able to deliver us.... But if not..."* When it comes to deliverance from sickness and disease, the Word of God is clear; He will deliver you and show you His salvation (Psalm 91). So, it is not right for a believer to say, *"God is able to heal me but if He does not..."* God will always heal. If you need healing and you ask God for it, you are in safe hands. He says in His Word, *"Ask and you will receive."* He does not say, *"Ask and then He may say yes, no, or wait,"* like some preachers have made their congregation believe. So, when you ask, according to His will, according to what has been revealed as yours, in the Word of God, you are welcome to start with thanksgiving and rejoicing thereafter. Because you will certainly receive.

Every promise and statement of fact that mentions what belongs to us, will be ours if we choose to act on what the Word of God says. For all the promises that have been expressed as ours, in the Word of God, you can pray the prayer of faith and make faith confessions, and you will surely receive what is rightfully yours in the Lord. For example, healing for your body is a statement of fact. You have been healed by the stripes of the Lord Jesus Christ (1 Peter 2:24). So, you need to pray in faith and receive what is rightfully yours in the Lord Jesus and do not make the statement, *"If God is willing,"* because God is always willing. The Bible says that the Son of man was manifested to destroy the works of the devil; sickness and disease are the works of the devil.

You must know in your heart that God is both willing and able to heal you and then make the confession with your mouth. A mental ascent to the fact that God is willing and able to heal you, will not do the job. You must believe in your heart. Belief in your heart comes with a careful study and meditation on the Word of God. That is why you must find at least two Scriptures that promise you what you are believing God for, and then start to meditate on them. Write them down and let them come out of your spirit and not just your mind. Do some reference checks, by referring to other Bible versions, Bible dictionaries, etc, for the Scriptures you are standing on. Listen to faith preachers who teach about how you can receive what you are desiring from God. Do this continually and never stop. This is what it means to pay attention to the Word of God, according to Proverbs 4:20. When I was believing God for the healing of my body, I continually listened to messages by brother Kenneth Copeland, Kenneth E Hagin, FF Bosworth and EW Kenyon. I drove to and from work, for about two hours every weekday. All that driving time was spent listening to these men of God, in my car. When I went to the gym for an hour, I would also listen to these faith preachers. This built my faith extensively.

Our faith in the Word of God is released through the confession of our mouths. The Christian life has been referred to as our confession, according to the New Testament.

Wherefore, holy brethren, partakers of the heavenly calling, consider the Apostle and High Priest of our profession, Christ Jesus.
Hebrew 3:1

Seeing then that we have a great high priest, that is passed into the heavens, Jesus the Son of God, let us hold fast our profession.
Hebrews 4:14

Let us hold fast the profession of our faith without wavering; (for he is faithful that promised.
Hebrews 10:23

We believe with our hearts and confess with our mouths. Your faith will raise you to the level of your confession. Therefore, when you understand the reality of who you are and what belongs to you, in the Lord Jesus Christ, you should make confessions of faith regarding those matters. It is not enough to only think about who you are; you must release your faith by declaring with your mouth about who you are.

You are healed because the Word of God says:

CHAPTER 9

Who his own self bare our sins in his own body on the tree, that we, being dead to sins, should live unto righteousness: by whose stripes ye were healed.
1 Peter 2:24 KJV

You have the wisdom to do anything that you are required to do in life because the Word of God says:

But of him are ye in Christ Jesus, who of God is made unto us wisdom, and righteousness, and sanctification, and redemption...
1 Corinthians 1:30

Confess these things to yourself. Let them become part of you and see the Lord Jesus work through you the most victorious accomplishments.

One thing I dread, is standing before God, one day, and looking back at areas where I failed to believe in Him and the things I could have done, if only I was courageous enough to dare God. Friends, let me encourage you to take God at His Word. Dare to believe God and do the things He said you must do, and expect Him to do the things He said He will do, in and through you, as you step up to do exploits for His glory.

BIBLIOGRAPHY

1. Albert Barnes' Notes on the Bible, 1847-85

2. W.E. Vine, Expository Dictionary of the New Testament Words, Zondervan Publishing House, 1952

OTHER BOOKS BY THE AUTHOR

KINGDOM FINANCE
The Tithe

YOU SHALL LIVE AND NOT DIE

MY NEW LIFE IN CHRIST